Anglo-Dutch Rivalry during the First Century
By George Edmundson

PREFACE

The varying fortunes of the obstinate and fiercely contested struggles with the Dutch for maritime and commercial supremacy in the days of the Commonwealth and the Restoration are familiar to all readers of English history, and especially of English naval history. Never did English seamen fight better than in these Dutch wars, and never did they meet more redoubtable foes. The details of the many dogged contests marked by alternate victory and defeat are now more or less unintelligible save to the expert in the naval strategy and tactics of the times, but legends have grown round the story of Martin Tromp sailing down the Channel with a broom at his mast-head, and of the exploit of Michael de Ruyter in burning the English ships at Chatham, which are never likely to be forgotten. The names of these two famous seamen are probably better known to Englishmen than those of any of the contemporary English admirals save that of Robert Blake alone. This fact should bespeak for the attempt that is here made to trace the causes and the growth of the Anglo-Dutch rivalry at sea and in commerce, which culminated in the collision between Blake and Tromp off Dover on May 29, 1652, and the declaration of war that followed. It has been my object in these Ford Lectures to treat of the relations between England and the United Provinces during the half-century that preceded the first outbreak of hostilities, and to make it clear that these wars of 1652-4, 1665-7, 1672-4 were the inevitable outcome of a long-continued clashing of interests, which were of fundamental importance and indeed vital to the welfare of both nations.

The first half of the seventeenth century was one of the most critical periods in English history. In any account of the reigns of the first two sovereigns of the House of Stewart political and religious questions of primary significance thrust themselves into the foreground of a picture full of deepening dramatic interest, with the result that other questions, apparently subordinate but in reality closely bound up with the national destinies, have been either relegated to the background or wholly overlooked and neglected. It has been so in regard to the questions dealt with in these pages.

The history of the revolt of the Netherlands and of the rise of the Dutch Republic shows to us Englishmen and Dutchmen united by bonds of sympathy and fighting side by side against a common foe. To both alike the Spaniard and the Inquisition were hateful, and in shedding their blood freely for the cause of Dutch freedom Englishmen were in fact acting in their own self-defence against the ambitious projects of Philip II. At first sight then it appears strange that the conclusion of the truce for twelve years in 1609 should have been followed by a coolness and growing estrangement in the relations between the two countries, and by a series of endless bickerings, grievances, and disputes which all the resources of diplomacy in protracted negotiations proved unable to settle amicably to the satisfaction of both parties. The truth is that the very points of resemblance in the racial characteristics of the English and the Dutch brought them into collision in almost every part of the world. Born colonizers, traders, and explorers, each people was instinctively conscious that its destiny was upon the water, and that mastery of the seas was a necessity of national existence. Hence a rivalry which was unavoidable, inexorable, a rivalry which could eventually have only one of two issues, either the voluntary submission of one of the rivals to the other, or a trial of strength by ordeal of battle.

James I and Charles I, whatever the deficiencies and mistakes of their foreign policies, were not blind to the significance of the appearance of this new sea-power on the other side of the 'narrow seas', and were quick to recognize that the Dutch menace to the essential interests of their island kingdom was at least as formidable as the Spanish menace had ever been. The diplomacy of both these kings was on the face of it vacillating, uncertain, and opportunist, but it is unjust to attribute this wholly to constitutional infirmity of purpose, or to an innate propensity to carry through their schemes by tortuous by-ways and dubious intrigues. There was no lack of steadfast determination on the part either of James or Charles in their resolute attempts to conduct the government and administration of their kingdoms autocratically without that adequate financial aid which Parliament alone could grant. But in consequence their treasury was generally empty, and it is therefore not surprising that, confronted with the constant fear of imminent bankruptcy, they were compelled to be shifty in their dealings with foreign powers, and to work for the achievement of their ends by the processes of a devious diplomacy rather than risk the costly charges of an appeal to arms. Nevertheless it will be seen that in their negotiations with the United Provinces never for a single moment would either James or Charles make the slightest concession in regard to the claims of the British Crown to undisputed sovereignty 'in the narrow seas', and they insisted that every foreign vessel should recognize that sovereignty by striking its flag when meeting a British war-ship in those waters.

The period with which I am dealing was one of chartered companies, of trade monopolies, and of commercial protection in its most aggressive form. Probably at that stage in the world's history no other economical system was conceivable or would have proved workable. In any case most of the disputes and differences between the English and the Dutch at this time arose from questions connected with trading privileges, and these lectures contain much concerning them. It is still, however, extremely interesting and not without instruction to read the arguments that were used and the principles that were upheld by these statesmen and diplomatists of former days. Economical questions are always with us, and men's opinions differ now as to their right solution as much as they did three centuries ago.

GEORGE EDMUNDSON.

11 SUMNER PLACE, S.W.

May 24, 1911.

———————————————————

I: 1600-1610

The last two decades of the sixteenth century hold a place apart in English History. The exploits of the great Elizabethan seamen helped to shatter the supremacy of Spain upon the sea, but they did more than this. They aroused in the English people the instinct of their true destiny, as a maritime, trading, and colonizing power. The granting of Charters to the Eastland (Baltic) Company (1579), to the Levant Company (1581), to the Guinea Company (1588), the foundation of the great East India Company (1600), the opening out by the Muscovy Company of a new trade route to Persia by way of Astrachan, the daring efforts to discover a North-West and a North-East passage to Cathay and the Indies, the first attempts to erect colonies in Virginia and Newfoundland, all testify to the spirit of enterprise which animated the nation, a spirit whose many-sided activity never failed to command the Queen's sympathy and encouragement. In thus entering, however, upon that path of colonial and commercial expansion which in later times was to become world-wide, the Englishman found himself in the first half of the seventeenth century confronted by a more formidable rival than the Spaniard. The defeat of the Invincible Armada was followed[1] by the rise of a new Sea-Power. At the opening of the seventeenth century the Dutch Republic had not only succeeded in resisting all the efforts made for its subjugation to Spanish rule, but, after more than thirty years of continuous and desperate struggle, was thriving in the midst of war. In the course of that struggle much help had been given, both in money and men, by Elizabeth. But the English Queen was not for many years whole-hearted in her support. She saw in the revolt of the Netherlands a means for draining the resources of a dangerous adversary. It was no small relief to her that the coast lying opposite to the mouth of the Thames, with its many ports and hardy sea-faring population, should no longer be at the disposal of the master of the strongest navy in the world. She felt a certain amount of sympathy with the Dutch on religious grounds, but a sympathy tempered by political considerations, and strictly subordinated to them. To support the rebellion of subjects against their legitimate ruler was to the instincts of the Tudor Queen a course which only necessity could justify. Hence her repeated refusal of the proffered sovereignty, her niggardly aid, her temporizing and apparently capricious attitude. As a matter of fact, throughout this critical period of her reign the policy of Elizabeth was not governed either by sentiment or by caprice. She always kept steadily in view the welfare and the security of England, with whose interests those of her own throne were identified, and she held aloof from entanglements which might be dangerous to the safety of her kingdom. Not until after the assassination of William the Silent, followed by the success of Parma in capturing Antwerp, August, 1585, did she make reply to the threatening attitude of Spain by openly taking sides with the rebel provinces. Still refusing the sovereignty, she sent Leicester at the head of a strong body of English troops to act in her name, as Governor-General, at the same time characteristically bargaining that the seaports

Flushing and Brill with the fort of Rammekens should be delivered to her in pledge for the repayment of her costs. The mission of Leicester was a failure, whether it be regarded from the military or the political standpoint, but it gave the Dutch at a transition period of disorganization and pressing peril a disciplined force to assist in their defence, and a breathing space for recuperation.

The resignation of his post by Leicester (April, 1588) may be taken as the date at which the history of the United Netherlands as a self-governing State really begins. The treaty with England still subsisted by the terms of which the Commander of the English auxiliary troops with two colleagues had seats in the Council of State, but the Council of State ceased ere long to have any but executive functions. The conduct of affairs affecting the whole Union was vested in the States-General as representing the States of the seven sovereign provinces from which its authority was derived. A more cumbrous system of government than that under which the United Provinces were now to develop rapidly into a powerful and flourishing State, probably never existed. That it was workable was due to two facts. The voices of the provinces were nominally of equal weight in the States-General, in reality that of Holland was dominant. Holland contributed 60 per cent. of the general expenses and contained about one-half of the entire population of the Union. With Zeeland she furnished almost the whole of the navy and was already becoming one of the most thriving centres of commerce in the world. At this time the influence of an exceptionally able statesman, John van Oldenbarneveldt, who filled the office of Advocate of Holland, was supreme in the States of that province, and as their representative and spokesman he was able to exercise an authority in the States-General which placed for thirty years in his hands the general administration of the country and the control of foreign affairs. By his side stood Maurice of Nassau, respected and honoured as the son of William the Silent, wielding as Captain and Admiral-General authority over all the armed forces of the Republic, and exercising as Stadholder of five provinces large executive powers. A consummate general but no politician, Maurice was content to leave the business of administration and the conduct of diplomacy in the hands of the statesman who had been his father's friend. Thus by the efforts of these two men, each eminent in his separate sphere, the youthful Republic, despite the inherent weaknesses of a confederacy so loosely compacted as that of the United Provinces, was able to carry out a wise and consistent foreign policy, to defend its borders, and meanwhile to thrive and flourish.

The relations between England and the States required the most careful handling during the whole of the period that intervened between the return of Leicester and the death of Elizabeth. The assistance given by the English Queen had not been without a return: it had been fully repaid by the services rendered by the Dutch fleet during the spring and summer of 1588 in blockading the ports in which lay the transports collected by the Duke of Parma for the invasion of England. When the Armada entered the Channel, Parma with his splendid veteran army was thus compelled to remain a helpless spectator of events, unable to take any part in promoting the success of the great enterprise which Philip had been so long preparing. But Elizabeth had been piqued by the opposition that Leicester had encountered, and by the evident determination of the States, under the leadership of Holland, not to permit any interference on the part of the representative of a foreign power with their provincial rights and privileges. She did not withdraw her help, but it was given from motives of pure self-interest rather than from any love for the cause she was supporting, and in a huckstering spirit. With her it was a question of give and take, and the military successes of Maurice, accompanied as they were by the rapid growth of commercial prosperity in Holland and Zeeland, only encouraged her to drive a harder bargain in her negotiations and to press for repayment of the loans she had advanced.

In these circumstances friction in the relations between England and the Republic was at times inevitable, but the community of interests was so strong that friendly co-operation never ceased. An English contingent took part in the campaigns of Maurice; a powerful Dutch squadron sailed with the fleet of Essex to the sack of Cadiz in 1595. The conclusion of peace between France and Spain in May, 1598, brought about a fresh treaty between England and the United Provinces, the terms of which point clearly to the great change which had taken place in the relative position of the two States since the time of Leicester's mission. The Dutch were now in a position to promise the repayment of their debt to Elizabeth by equal annual instalments[3] and to undertake in case of a Spanish attack upon England to come to the assistance of their allies with thirty ships of war and a force of 5,000 infantry and five cornets of cavalry. On the other hand, only one Englishman henceforth was to have a seat upon the Council of State, and the English auxiliary troops in the Netherlands were transferred to the service of the States as their paymasters and were required to take an oath of allegiance to them. This English brigade in the Dutch service, now first formed, was to have a long and honourable career. It was speedily to prove its worth and gain immortal fame by the share that it took in winning the great victory of Nieuwport (July 2, 1600), and in the heroic defence of Ostend (1601-4).

Such was the state of things when James I ascended the English throne. From him the Netherlands could hope for little active aid. The chief aim of James's policy from the first was to live on friendly terms with Spain, and in 1604 he concluded a treaty of peace with Philip III and with the Archdukes, as sovereigns of the Netherlands. His attitude to the United Provinces was not indeed unfriendly. He still retained the cautionary towns, as a pledge for the debt, and his representative sat in the Council of State, but as one of the conditions of peace he promised to lend no assistance to the Dutch. The privilege of recruiting in England for the regiments in their service was not withdrawn, but in return a like privilege was extended to the Spaniards. Thus there were occasions on which Englishmen were found fighting against one another on opposite sides. The Court of Madrid on their part, exhausted by the long and costly struggle, were already in 1606 making tentative proposals to the rebel provinces for the conclusion of a peace or truce, and meanwhile spared no efforts to prejudice the mind of James against a people for whose cause as a stanch Protestant it was feared he might have secret leanings, and at the same time to secure his benevolent support in the coming negotiations. The arguments that were used and their effect upon the King are well summed up in the words of the keen-eyed Venetian Ambassador, Nicolò Molin, who in 1607 thus reports:—

'The Spaniards are ceaselessly urging upon the King that for his own interests he ought to use his utmost endeavours in this negotiation in order to bring it to some conclusion, since by continuance of the war the Dutch might come to make themselves masters of those seas. Having their fleets ordinarily of a hundred or more ships, and these widely scattered in different places, they can thus say, and with truth, that they are masters of those seas for the possession of which the ancient kings of England have made very long and very costly wars against the princes of Europe. The King knows all this to be true, but is likewise of opinion that at a single nod of his the Dutch would yield to him all that dominion that they have gained; which without doubt would follow so long as the war with the Spaniards lasted, since they are not able at one and the same time to contend with two of the greatest princes of Christendom. But if with time that ripens affairs peace should be effected between them and the Crown of Spain, I do not know if they would be so ready to yield as the King of England promises himself; since just as this profession of the sea is manifestly more and more on the wane in England, so more and more is it increasing and acquiring force and vigour among the Dutch.'

The perspicacity of this review of the situation was completely justified by the events. On April 9, 1609, after prolonged and acrimonious negotiations, a treaty for a truce of twelve years between the belligerents was signed, but on conditions imposed by the Dutch. To the Spaniards the terrible drain on their resources made a respite from war a matter not of choice, but of necessity. To obtain it they had to treat with the United Provinces 'as if they were an independent State', and, worst of all, they had by a secret clause to concede liberty of trading in the Indies. From this moment the relations of the States with England were sensibly changed. The attitude of King James had hitherto been a mixture of condescension and aloofness, and he had not troubled himself to consider seriously the question of Dutch rivalry upon the seas and in commerce, which had so profoundly impressed the Venetian envoy. Nicolò Molin was in 1607 undoubtedly correct in his supposition that at that date James still looked upon the Dutch as dependents on his favour, who would not venture to run counter to any expression of his will. The course of the negotiations for the truce must have gradually undeceived him, and their issue left him face to face with a power compelled to maintain to the utmost the interests of the extensive commerce on the proceeds of which its very existence as a State depended.

No sooner were the signatures appended to the treaty than James took a step which exposed to a very severe strain his relations with the people whose emancipation from Spanish rule he had, ostensibly at least, worked hard to accomplish. Many indeed in Holland had been suspicious of the real friendliness of his attitude during the negotiations, but very few probably imagined that he was preparing, as soon as they were ended, to put to the test their sense of the value of his services and of his alliance by striking a deadly blow at the most important of their industries. On May 16, 1609, the King issued a proclamation, in which, after stating that though he had hitherto tolerated the promiscuous liberty that had been granted to foreigners to fish in the British seas, he has now determined, seeing that this liberty

'hath not only given occasion of over great Encroachments upon our Regalities, or rather questioning of our Right, but hath been a means of daily Wrongs to our own People that exercise the Trade of Fishing... to give notice to all the World that our express Pleasure is, that from the beginning of the Month of August next coming, no Person of what Nation or Quality soever, be permitted to fish upon any of our Coasts and Seas of Great Britain, Ireland and the rest of the Isles adjacent, until they have orderly demanded and obtain'd Licences from us....'

The news of the publication of this edict caused in Holland no small surprise, not unmingled with indignation. On June 12 the matter was discussed in the States of that Province, and it was resolved[3] that the States-General be requested to adopt measures for the vigorous defence of the land's rights as based upon the treaties. The States-General on their part resolved[4] that a full inquiry should be made into the question of treaty rights and a special embassy be sent to London, and as early as July 6, King James agreed[5] to receive such a deputation, and to appoint commissioners to enter into conference with it on the subject of the privileges and immunities for freedom of commerce claimed in virtue of ancient treaties. Meanwhile the States-General promised the fishermen their protection, at the same time bidding them to be very careful not to give any cause for new complaints on the part of the King. So far indeed were the Dutch from yielding immediate submission to the demand of James, or from admitting its justice, that Sir Ralph Winwood (the resident English ambassador at the Hague), reporting to the Secretary of State, Lord Salisbury, the results of an interview he had had with Oldenbarneveldt September 16, 1609, informs him:—

'the States do write expressly to their ambassador [Noel Caron] urging him to advertise his Majesty their purpose to send to beseech him upon the necessity of this affair [i.e. liberty of fishing] in the meantime to have patience with their people trading upon his coast that without impeachment they may use *their accustomed Liberty and antient Privelidges*; which he [Oldenbarneveldt] said they were so far from fear that his Majesty upon due consideration will abridge, as that they hope he will be pleased to inlarge and increase into new ones.'[6]

For a right understanding of the importance of the fisheries question and of the reasons which led King James at this particular time to issue his proclamation, a short retrospect is necessary.

Special rights of free fishing in English waters had been granted to the Hollanders and Zeelanders, as early as 1295, by King Edward I, and afterwards renewed by several of his successors. Finally a treaty was concluded, dated February 24, 1496, known as the *Magnus Intercursus*, between Henry VII and Philip the Fair, Duke of Burgundy, which was destined to regulate the commercial relations between England and the Netherlands during the whole of the Tudor period, and was still in force in 1609. Article XIV of this treaty ran as follows:—

'Conventum, concordatum et conclusum est quod Piscatores utriusque Partis Partium praedictarum (cujuscunque conditionis existant) poterunt ubique Ire, Navigare per Mare, secure Piscari absque aliquo Impedimento, Licentia, seu Salvo Conductu.'

Nothing could be more explicit or complete, and it was to this clause of the *Magnus Intercursus* and the rights it had so long recognized that Oldenbarneveldt referred when he spoke to Winwood of the Dutch fishermen's 'accustomed Liberty and antient Privelidges.'

The rights of the Netherlanders to trade and navigate in Scottish waters, 'sine aliquo salvo conductu aut licentia generali aut speciali', were guaranteed by the Treaty of Binche, dated December 15, 1550, which had been confirmed by James himself, as King of Scotland, in 1594. But neither in this treaty of 1550, nor in an earlier treaty of 1541 to which it expressly refers, '*circa Piscationem et liberum usum Maris, ea quae per Tractatum anno 1541... inita, conclusa ac conventa fuerint debite ac sincere observari debebunt*', is there any definite statement that the free use of the sea carried with it the right to fish without payment, though undoubtedly that right seems to be implied, and was certainly exercised without let or hindrance before 1609.

The question at issue was of vital consequence to the Dutch. It may be asserted without any exaggeration that the commerce and prosperity of Holland and Zeeland had been built upon the herring fishery, and rested upon it. The discovering of the art of curing the herring by Willem Beukelsz at the close of the fourteenth century had transformed a perishable article of local consumption into a commodity for traffic and exchange. Soon the 'great fishery', as it was called, afforded, directly or indirectly, occupation and a means of livelihood to a large part of the entire population of the Province of Holland.[7] Not only did many thousands of Hollanders put out to sea to follow the track of the herring shoals along the British coasts, but thousands more found employment on shore in building the busses, pinks, and other boats engaged in the lucrative industry, and in providing them with ropes, nets, and other necessaries. The profit from the fishery alone before the outbreak of the revolt was estimated by Guicciardini at 500,000 Flemish pounds. But such an estimate was far from representing the real value of what was styled by the States-General in an official document 'one of the chiefest mines of the United Netherlands'.[8] Salt was required for the curing. It was brought in Dutch bottoms in its rough state from French and Spanish ports, or direct from Punta del Rey on the coast of Venezuela, and salt-refineries quickly sprang up at Enkhuysen, Hoorn, and other fishing centres. In a land which had no natural products, the cured herrings and the refined salt which were not required for home use served as articles of commerce, and freights were dispatched to the neighbouring lands but specially to the Baltic to be exchanged for corn, timber, hemp, and other 'Eastland' commodities. The enterprising Hollanders and Zeelanders, at first competed with the Hanse towns in the Baltic ports, but long before the opening of the seventeenth century had practically driven their rivals from the field, and at the time with which we are dealing it has been computed that no less than 3,000 Dutch vessels were engaged in the 'Eastland' traffic through the Sound. The corn in its turn brought by so vast a fleet far more than sufficed even for the needs of a country where no corn was grown. Some thousands of other ships laden with grain voyaged along the coast of France, the Peninsula and the Western Mediterranean, discharging their cargoes and returning with freights of wine, silk, olive oil, and other staple products of the South. The Spaniards and Portuguese were in fact largely dependent upon the Hollanders for their necessary food supplies, and these keen traders had no scruples in enriching themselves at the cost of their foes. An abundance of timber and hemp also came from the Baltic and furnished the raw material for flourishing shipbuilding and ropemaking industries. Sawmills sprang up on the banks of the Zaan, and before long Zaandam became the chief centre of the timber trade of Europe. It will thus be seen at once how many Dutch interests were involved in the full maintenance of the rights to free fishing on the British coasts guaranteed by treaty, and why it was that the States-General under pressure from the States of Holland should have determined to send a special embassy to protest strongly and firmly against the edict of King James, and should have meantime promised the fishermen their protection in case of any attempt being made to compel them by armed force to pay the licences.

The step taken by King James had, however, from the English point of view much to recommend it. The English people saw the growing maritime strength and rapidly increasing commercial prosperity of the Dutch with jealous eyes. Their practical monopoly of the British fisheries was deeply resented. Pamphlets were written lamenting the decadence of English shipping and trade.[9] It was felt that the ancient claim of England to the sovereignty and dominion of the narrow seas was being challenged, and that its maintenance depended upon the numbers and the experience of the sea-faring population, for whom the fisheries were the best and most practical school. A petition is extant from the fishermen of the Cinque Ports to the King, showing that the Netherlanders drive them from their fishing, and sell fresh fish contrary to the laws, and beseeching His Majesty to impose on them a tax of fifteen shillings upon every last of fish, the same as they imposed on the English.[10]James was far from indisposed to listen to their complaints. Early in his reign, in 1604, an attempt had been made to enforce the eating of fish in England on fast-days, and the motive of it was plainly stated. It had little to do with religious observances. It was 'for the better increase of Seamen, to be readie at all times to serve in the Kings Majesties Navie, of which the fishermen of England have euer been the chiefest Seminarie and Nurserie.'[11] The suggestion that licences should be required for which a tax or toll should be paid naturally presented itself to the King, at this time in sore straits for money and at his wit's end how to obtain it, as a welcome expedient. It also afforded a means by which the sovereignty and jurisdiction of the British King in the British seas could be asserted and his regalities safeguarded.[12]The large revenue derived by Christian IV of Denmark from the tolls in the Sound had no doubt often made the impecunious James envious of his brother-in-law, whose right to levy such an import in Danish waters differed in no way from the right, which as King of Great Britain and Ireland he was now asserting, to demand a licence from all foreigners who desired to fish on the

British coasts. His decision to issue the proclamation was confirmed by the appearance in March, 1609, of the famous treatise of Hugo Grotius, entitled *Mare Liberum*. The argument in this work seemed to be directed against the principle of a *dominium maris* such as the English Kings had claimed for centuries in the 'narrow seas', and its publication at this time aroused the resentment of James, always tenaciously jealous of any infringement of his sovereign prerogatives. As a matter of fact, as has been shown by the late Professor Robert Fruin[13], the *Mare Liberum* was originally a chapter of a larger unpublished work of Grotius, written to prove that the Portuguese had no exclusive rights in the Indian Ocean but that the Eastern seas and all others were open to the traders of every nation. The most burning question in the negotiations for the twelve years' truce, then just drawing to a close, had been that of the liberty to trade in the Indies, demanded with insistence by the Dutch, refused up to the very last peremptorily by the Spanish King, and conceded by him finally not directly but by a kind of subterfuge. The *Mare Liberum* of Grotius saw the light at a time when it was hoped that his learned arguments might tend to allay the acuteness of the dispute by showing the reasonableness and legality of the position taken up by the Dutch. It is clear now that these arguments, though their application was general, had their special reference to Portuguese and not to British pretensions. Curiously enough, as will be seen later, it was in the long succession of Anglo-Dutch negotiations over the fisheries in the seas over which the Crown of England claimed paramount sovereignty and jurisdiction that the thesis put forward by the author of the *Mare Liberum* was destined to be the source of embittered controversy. The acute mind of King James was quick in grasping its importance.

Delayed by various causes, it was not till April 16, 1610, that the embassy from the States set sail from Brill for England. The object of the mission was ostensibly a complimentary one—to thank the King for the active part he had taken, as a mediator, in bringing the truce negotiations to a favourable issue. The two matters which called for serious discussion were: (1) the critical situation which had arisen in the Jülich-Cleves Duchies owing to a disputed succession; (2) the proclamation about the fisheries. The importance of the last question was revealed by the fact that all the five envoys originally selected were representatives of the two maritime provinces. One of the five died at Brill just before starting. The four who actually sailed (April 16) were: Johan Berck, pensionary of Dort; Albert de Veer, pensionary of Amsterdam; Elias van Oldenbarneveldt, pensionary of Rotterdam; and a Zeelander, Albert Joachimi, who was later to show himself a skilful diplomatist during the twenty-five years that he was resident Dutch ambassador in London. Elias van Oldenbarneveldt was the brother of the Advocate of Holland. According to a letter from Sir Ralph Winwood[14] to Lord Salisbury he had special charge of the fishery question, a proof of the peculiar interest felt by the Advocate in the issue raised. With them was joined the resident ambassador, Noel Caron. Their instructions required them to seek from His Majesty an explanation of his intentions in the proclamation, 'since their High Mightinesses the

States-General could not believe that he meant to include the inhabitants of the United Netherlands among those who were bidden to pay for a licence to fish, since this was contrary to the ancient treaties subsisting between them and the Crowns of England and Scotland. After audiences with the King (April 27) and with the Privy Council (May 8), it was arranged that a Conference on the fisheries question should be held, with a Committee of the Council, two of whose members were Sir Julius Caesar, Chancellor of the Exchequer, and Sir Thomas Parry, Chancellor of the Duchy of Lancaster. The Conference opened on May 16, and the points in dispute were argued at length. The Dutch case was presented in a memorandum drawn up with much skill, probably by the hand of Hugo Grotius himself. The freedom of fishing was claimed on two grounds: (1) that of the privileges granted by ancient treaties still in force; (2) that of abstract right, because the sea, like the air, is for the common use of all and cannot be private property. The weak point of the case lay in the fact that these two grounds, that of treaty right and that of the *Mare Liberum*, seemed to be in a certain sense contradictory. The English, however, would not admit that the question of the immemorial claim of the Kings of England to sovereignty and jurisdiction in the seas adjoining the British coasts was open to discussion, and seizing upon the argument placed in their hands by the Dutch memorandum itself, pleaded with great force that the granting of privileges implied the power to take them away or modify them, should the King deem such a step necessary to protect the interests of his own subjects. The Conference therefore effected nothing more than the bringing out in relief of the differences of view of the two parties. But reflection brought wisdom. There was no wish on either side to press matters to extremities. Already on May 10 the States-General, unwilling to run the risk of making James an enemy, at a time when they were very anxious to secure his help in the settlement of the Jülich-Cleves succession question[15], had sent instructions to their ambassadors not to make difficulties or unpleasantness about the fisheries, but rather to propose that the execution of the proclamation should be postponed for two years, in order that the question might be thoroughly investigated. There were several claimants to the Jülich-Cleves inheritance, Protestant and Catholic, and it was of vital importance to the States, and also to a lesser extent to all Protestant princes in Germany and to James, that this frontier territory on the Rhine should not fall under the rule of a Catholic sovereign. But the Archduke Leopold had seized the fortress of Jülich, and Henry IV of France, jealous of the power of the House of Habsburg in Europe, had put himself at the head of a coalition to secure the succession to the Elector of Brandenburg, and William, Count Palatine of Neuburg, as joint possessors. There was a general desire to avoid hostilities, but Henry IV had pushed forward his preparations for a great campaign, and war seemed inevitable. At this moment the assassination of the French king at the very time the Conference was being held in London changed the whole aspect of affairs. The new French Government was favourably disposed to Spain. The Dutch therefore were left face to face with the task of expelling the Archduke from

Jülich, and they felt that all other matters were for the moment of secondary importance to that of having the friendly co-operation of James in case of the outbreak of war. Their attitude to the fisheries question was therefore considerably modified. It became much more conciliatory, and for precisely similar reasons a like change took place in the attitude of the English King. He too felt that the friendship of the Dutch was essential to him at such a critical juncture, and at a meeting with the Earls of Salisbury and Northampton, May 24, the Dutch envoys were agreeably surprised to find that the King, while not formally abating one jot of his sovereign rights in the matter of issuing licences for fishing, was willing to postpone the execution of his edict for two years. The ambassadors took leave of the King the same day and started on their return journey. Of this audience the Lords of the Council, in a letter to Winwood, dated May 18, 1610 (o.s.), write:

'For the States Ambassadors, His Majesty is now dismissing them with sufficient assurance of his inward affections towards them and the preservation of their State, which next to his own he holdeth most dear above all other respects in the world. And as for the matter of fishing and Reglement of commerce, His Majesty thinketh not fit now to spend any more time in it, but to refer the one and the other to some better season; and in the meanwhile that things may remain in the same state as now they are. So as we conceive these Deputies will return with good contentment, having no other cause either for the public or for the private; and His Majesty having also been careful to give them the rights that appertain to their title, and all other external courtesy and honour in their reception.'

This good understanding was to bear good fruit. The army, which Maurice of Nassau led into the duchy in June, contained a fine body of English troops under the command of Sir Edward Cecil. Jülich was besieged and surrendered to the Dutch on September 1, and the Archduke Leopold was compelled to leave the territory. Of this achievement Sir Ralph Winwood, writing to Lord Salisbury from Dusseldorf, August 22 (o.s.), says: 'The honor of the conduct of this seige no man will detract from the Count Maurice, who is the *Maistre-ouvrier* in that *Mestier*. But that this Seige hath had so happy an end, himself will and doth attribute it to the Diligence and Judgement of Sir Edward Cecil.' The capture of Jülich did not indeed end this thorny little dispute. Anglo-Dutch and Spanish-Imperial armies, under Maurice and Spinola respectively, manœuvred within a short distance of one another. But the quarrel was localized, no further hostilities took place, and finally by the Treaty of Xanten, November 12, 1614, an arrangement was arrived at. During all this time the relations between James and the States were friendly. The King, however, had quarrelled with his Parliament, and even had he wished to take a stronger line in foreign politics, lack of funds compelled him to temporize. The English contingent in Maurice's army was recruited indeed in England, but the troops were in the pay of the States. Moreover, James was all the time hankering after a Spanish marriage for the Prince of Wales, from mixed motives doubtless, but chiefly from a misguided notion that such an alliance between the leading Catholic and the leading Protestant State would enable him to play the part of arbiter in the religious differences which were dividing Europe into two hostile camps, and by his influence to prevent an actual breach of the peace. This was the underlying motive which prompted all the apparent fluctuations of his policy. Hence the persistence with which for so many years he pursued the *chimaera* of a Spanish match, while at the same time he allowed his only daughter to marry the Elector Palatine, the head of the Protestant Union in Germany, and endeavoured to maintain good relations with the United Provinces, notwithstanding the continual friction between his subjects and the Dutch regarding the increasing monopoly by the latter of the fisheries and of sea-borne trade. The situation in 1611 is thus described by the Venetian, Marcantonio Correr[16]:—

'With the lords of the United Provinces of the Low Countries, there exists at present perfect friendship and union; formerly he [James] used to despise them, as rebels, but now he loves and esteems them, as princes of valour and quality, an effect of the truce made with the Catholic king.... Now H.M. desires and procures the preservation of the Dutch, but not a further increase of their greatness, since their forces on sea are not inferior to those of any potentate whatsoever, because that in time of war necessity has been their best mistress. Of these forces the English are not without some jealousy, seeing their own diminished, and the dominion of the sea, that they have been accustomed to hold in that part of the ocean transferred to others.... In the herring fishery alone they [the Dutch] send out every year to the east coast of the Kingdom of England 1,700 vessels, in which perhaps 30,000 men are employed.[17] After the truce the King made a proclamation, that no one was allowed to fish in those parts without licence, perhaps incited by the great sums of money, that formerly the Spaniards offered Queen Elizabeth to have the user of it; but just as at that time that scheming did not succeed in despoiling the Dutch, so now these with two special ambassadors have not obtained any promise of an alteration, as he [the King] is always intent upon the conservation of his jurisdiction and the increase of the royal incomings. The King at present regards the possession of such great sea power as being in itself of great moment for the needs of England, and united with his own it could with difficulty be resisted. He holds further that these same provinces are a barrier rampart of his kingdoms, and he is interested in them through the debt of a million and a half of gold that remains to him of the sum of more than two millions already lent by Queen Elizabeth, the repayment of which is at present spread over a number of years, a portion every year. Meanwhile three principal places are pledges in the hands of his Majesty....'

The possession of these fortresses was indeed at this time placing King James in a position of no small advantage in his dealings with the States, and he was well aware of it. On the other hand, it was galling to the Dutch, now that they had compelled the Spaniard to treat with the United Provinces as if it were an independent State, to feel that two chief doors of entrance into their land were in the hands of foreign garrisons. James professed to be their good friend, and it appeared to be his interest to cultivate their alliance, but it was inevitable that his assiduous advances to gain the goodwill of Spain and to obtain the hand of an Infanta for his son should render him suspect.

II: 1610-1618

The resolve of the King in 1610 to postpone any action in the matter of his proclamation on the fisheries question seems not to have aroused any popular expression of disapproval. The English people were from the political and religious standpoint well disposed to the Dutch. What they suspected and dreaded was the King's obvious leaning to Spain. Their intense dislike to the Spanish marriage, concerning which it was common knowledge that negotiations were on foot, led them to favour a good understanding with the United Provinces. But the spectacle of the growing Dutch monopoly of the carrying trade, and the decline of English commerce in the face of these formidable rivals, could not fail before long to stir public opinion.

A succession of noteworthy pamphlets drew attention to the subject. Foremost among these, from the personality of the writer, was Ralegh's[18] *Observations touching trade and commerce with the Hollanders and others, wherein is proved that our sea and land commodities serve to enrich and strengthen other countries than our own.* These *Observations* were, as the title page informs us, presented to King James, and there are indications that the date of their presentation was about the time of the Dutch embassy of 1610. Their object was to show how Dutch trade was prospering at the expense of that of England. Ralegh pointed out in particular the immense profit derived by the Hollanders from their fishing in the British seas, and he asks why 'this great sea-business of fishing' should not be kept in English hands, and suggests that the King should appoint Commissioners to inquire into the matter, and 'forthwith set forward some scheme for preventing foreigners from reaping all the fruits of this lucrative industry on his Majesty's coasts.' He warns the King that 'the Hollanders possess already as many ships as eleven kingdoms, England being one of them', and expresses his conviction that 'they [the Hollanders] hoped to get the whole trade and shipping of Christendom into their own hands, as well for transportation, as otherwise for the command and mastery of the seas.'

Ralegh's pamphlet did not affect the King's decision to defer, for political reasons, taking any active steps concerning the fisheries, but we may well believe that the hint about 'the command and mastery of the seas' would not pass unheeded. It touched a question about which James was peculiarly sensitive. That question, though for a few years apparently dormant, was one that neither King nor people could afford to disregard. The command of the sea—then as at all times—was vital to an island power. The English were beginning to see in the Dutch not merely competitors in trade, who were ousting them from every market, but possible rivals for the dominion even of those 'narrow seas[19]' in which the Kings of England had so long claimed to have paramount sovereignty and jurisdiction. Thus a feeling of dissatisfaction and resentment gathered head which found vent, as was the custom of those days, in political pamphlet-writing. Two of these pamphlets[20], no less than that of Ralegh, call for particular notice, for they are full of material bearing upon the subject of the relations between the English and Dutch at the time of their publication, and throwing light upon the causes of the growing estrangement between the two people.

England's Way to win Wealth, by Tobias Gentleman, Fisherman and Mariner, bears the date 1614. The purpose of the writer is thoroughly practical. He sets out in great detail the statistics of the fisheries on the British coasts, and of the immense profits derived by the Hollanders from the pursuit of this industry, and he then proceeds to urge upon his countrymen to take a lesson from the foreigners, and not to neglect, as they are doing, a source of wealth which lies at their very doors. The following quotation is a good specimen of the homely vigour and directness of Gentleman's arguments; it will be seen that here, as throughout the pamphlet, they profess to be based on his own personal experience:—

'What their [the Hollanders] chiefest trade is, or their principal gold mine is well known to all merchants, that have used those parts, and to myself and all fishermen; namely, that his Majesty's seas is their chiefest, principal, and only rich treasury whereby they have so long maintained their wars, and have so greatly prospered and enriched themselves. If their little country of the United Provinces can do this (as is most manifest before our eyes they do) then what may we, his Majesty's subjects, do, if this trade of fishing were once erected among us, we having, in our own countries, sufficient store of all necessaries to accomplish the like business?... And shall we neglect so great blessings, O slothful England and careless countrymen! Look but on these fellows, that we call the plump Hollanders, behold their diligence in fishing and our own careless negligence.'[21]

Another pamphlet, *The Trades Increase* [22], was of wider scope. It was directly inspired, as its anonymous author J. R. informs us, by the reading of *England's Way to win Wealth*. It deals not only with the question of the fisheries, but of shipping and trade generally, and rightly with shipping first of all. 'As concerning ships,' J. R. writes—and how true do his words ring in an Englishman's ears to-day—'by these in a manner we live, the kingdom is, the King reigneth.... If we want ships, we are dissolved.' As Gentleman's pamphlet is valuable for its detailed statistics of the fishing industry of the Hollanders, even more so is that of J. R. for its broad survey of and comparison between the Dutch and English trade in every part of the world. From country to country and sea to sea in all branches of commerce he shows how the English are being driven out by their more enterprising competitors.

'In consequence want of employment is breeding discontents and miseries, while the means for remedying threatened disaster are in our own hands, the place our own seas and within his Majesty's dominions.'

Nor is J. R. content with mere assertion. Basing his arguments on those of Gentleman, he proceeds to set forth how by the encouragement of English fishing

'we shall repair our Navy, breed seamen abundantly, enrich the subject, advance the King's custom, and assure the Kingdom, and all this out of fishing and especially out of herrings.'

As to the Hollanders, he remarks significantly:—

'Howsoever it pleaseth his Majesty to allow of his royal predecessor's bounty, in tolerating the neighbour nations to fish in his streams, yet other princes take more straight courses.'

This powerful and reasoned summary of a condition of affairs so threatening to

England's supremacy as a maritime power, and to the welfare of her people, testifies to the mixture of indignation and alarm with which the English people regarded the rapid progress in commerce and wealth of 'their neighbours the new Sea-Herrs', as J. R. names the Dutch. If further evidence were wanting as to the state of feeling in the country, it is furnished by the striking language of the Venetian envoy, Pietro Contarini (1617/18). According to the report of this impartial observer[23]:—

'Loud praises of past times and the worthy deeds of forefathers form the topic of conversation. I have heard great lords with tears of the deepest affliction lamenting the present state of things and grieving how England has already fallen in reputation with all the world, England whose name and whose forces were feared by foes and esteemed by friends. Now the memory of past glory lost, as it were fallen into forgetfulness of herself, she abandons not only the interests of others, but even her own.'

Such was the result of the forciful feeble policy of James, striving to pose as the keeper of the peace of Europe, and to hold the balance between the rival forces of Catholicism and Protestantism already arming for the terrible struggle of the Thirty Years' War. After the marriage of his only daughter with the head of the Protestant Union in Germany, he was soon once more in eager pursuit of the phantasmal Spanish match, which was for so many years to make him follow a vacillating policy. The skilful diplomacy of Diego Sarmiento d'Acuña, Count of Gondomar, who represented Philip III in London after 1613, enabled him at this time to acquire a great ascendancy over James, which with brief intervals he maintained for some years. The Spanish envoy left no steps untried in the course of the disputes which arose with the United Provinces to prejudice the King's mind against the Dutch. He found the moment peculiarly favourable for making his influence felt, and he used his opportunities to the utmost. It must be remembered that the year 1612, in which first Robert Cecil, Lord Salisbury, died, and then six months later Henry, Prince of Wales, a youth of great promise and popularity, whose strong personality must have impressed itself on the history of his times, is a critical dividing point in the reign of James I. Ranke has in his account of this period laid considerable stress on this fact:—

'In the first years of his reign in England', he writes, 'so long as Robert Cecil lived, King James exercised no great influence. The Privy Council possessed to the full the authority, which belonged to it of old custom. James used simply to confirm the resolutions, which were adopted in the bosom of the Council under the influence of the treasurer. He appears in the reports of ambassadors as a phantom King, and the minister as the real ruler of the country. After the death of Cecil all this was changed. The King knew the party divisions which prevailed in the Council; he knew how to hold the balance between them, and in the midst of their divisions to carry out his views.... Great affairs were generally transacted between the King and the favourite in the ascendant at the time in conferences to which only a few others were admitted, and sometimes not even these. The King himself decided, and the resolutions that were taken were communicated to the Privy Council, which gradually became accustomed to do nothing more than invest them with the customary forms.'[24]

It was at this very time, when King James, yielding himself more and more to the persuasive blandishments of Gondomar, began to take a more markedly personal part in the direction of foreign policy, that a succession of fresh difficulties with the Dutch arose. The execution of the proclamation, which had been deferred for two years in 1610, actually remained a dead letter until 1616. Not that there had been any removal of the causes which had originally called it forth. On the contrary, the first years of the truce were a period of marked activity and vigorous forward policy in the United Provinces. In every direction, through the energetic and vigilant statesmanship of Oldenbarneveldt, the commercial enterprise of the people was enabled to open out fresh outlets for trade, and finally to secure the recognition of the young Republic as an influential member of the European family of nations. Diplomatic missions were dispatched to Venice in 1609 and to Constantinople in 1612, which prepared the way for a great extension of Dutch trade in the Eastern Mediterranean. Even more important were the close relations established with Sweden and Russia. Göteburg became after 1609 virtually a Dutch town, and before the middle of the century all Swedish industries and Swedish commerce had passed more or less into Dutch management or under Dutch control. In the reign of Elizabeth the friendliest relations had subsisted with the Tsar, Ivan the Terrible and his successors, so that for some years the English Muscovy Company had almost a monopoly of Russian trade by the White Sea. But all this was now changed. A famous Dutch merchant, Balthazar de Moncheron, established a factory at Archangel in 1584, and from that time forward the Dutch, at first vigorous competitors with the English for the Russian market, gradually gained the supremacy. The appearance of a Russian embassy at the Hague in 1614 was the mark of the triumph of Dutch diplomacy at Moscow: henceforth Russia was practically closed to all but Netherlanders. In 1615 a treaty with the Hanse towns placed the Baltic trade even more completely than it had been in Dutch hands. In the East Indies the English Company could not compete with its far wealthier and more thoroughly organized rival.

There was, however, one element of weakness in the position of the United Provinces on which the English were never weary of insisting. By his possession of the cautionary towns the King of England appeared in the eyes of the world to be recognized as a protector of the Dutch Republic, who had certain rights over it. Oldenbarneveldt in his negotiations had doubtless been hampered by the plain evidence which the presence of English garrisons in Flushing, Brill, and Rammekens afforded, that the States did not exercise full sovereign authority within their own borders. In these circumstances he (Oldenbarneveldt) knowing full well the financial straits to which King James was reduced through the long-standing disagreement between him and his Parliament, made overtures in 1615 through the resident ambassador Caron to redeem the towns by the payment of a sum of ready money. The annual charge of £40,000 received from the States was barely more than sufficient for the maintenance of the garrisons. The total amount claimed by the English Government was £600,000; the Dutch offered £100,000 in cash, and three further sums of £50,000 in half-yearly instalments, or £250,000 in all. The offer was accepted and in June, 1616, the cautionary towns were transferred into the hands of the Dutch.

It was, however, agreed that, for the sake of maintaining good relations between the two countries, the new English ambassador, Sir Dudley Carleton, should like his predecessor, Sir Ralph Winwood, retain his seat in the Council of State. This was the more important, as the King had (as already stated) for the past three years been steadily moving towards a Spanish alliance. What were his precise aims and what his ultimate purpose it was difficult even for the practised and penetrating insight of a statesman of Oldenbarneveldt's experience to discover. Perhaps James scarcely knew himself. But the retention of fortresses like Flushing and Brill at the mouths of two most important Dutch waterways by a foreign sovereign, who was intriguing to win the favour of the Spanish foe, was for the Republic a most serious danger. Their redemption therefore at so trifling a cost was a stroke of policy by which the aged Advocate did a great service to his country. Certain it is that James felt a grudge against Oldenbarneveldt, and that, when shortly afterwards civil strife broke out in the United Provinces, Sir D. Carleton, acting on the King's instructions, did his utmost to bring about the great statesman's downfall and to support his enemies in compassing his death.

But to return. Sir Dudley Carleton, when entering upon his duties at the Hague in January, 1616, found, in addition to the negotiations for the 'reddition' of the cautionary towns, several thorny questions requiring delicate handling. In his instructions[25] the following somewhat enigmatical passage occurs:—

'Some two years since there did arise between the Company of our Muscovy Merchants and the Merchants of Amsterdam a great difference concerning the navigation of Greenland[26] and the fishing of whales in those parts. Our desire is that all good correspondence may be maintained, as between our Crowns and their Provinces, so between our and their subjects. Therefore, whenever the subject shall fall into discourse, either in public or in private, you may confidently relate, when this question was debated before the lords of the Council, between Sir Noel Caron their embassador and the Governor of our Muscovian Company, it was evidently proved, and in a manner without contradiction, that our subjects were first discoverers of that negotiation and that trade of fishing; that privately they were possessed of that island, and had planted and erected our standard, thereby to signify and notify to the world the property, which we challenge; which our subjects, by their industries, having appropriated to themselves, did not hold it reasonable they should be forced to communicate to others the fruits of their labours.'

The origin and cause of this new fishery dispute requires to be briefly told, as it is characteristic of the times and of the way in which, in almost every part of the world, the English trader and the Dutch trader met in rivalry, and with the inevitable result that their interests clashed and bad feeling arose. Certain English fishing vessels as early as 1608 made their way to the Arctic Ocean to fish for whales off the shores of Spitzbergen. The adventure was successful, and was repeated. The news of it attracted some Biscayans, then other foreigners, and in 1612 two Dutch ships to try their fortune in the same waters. But King James in the following year (1613) granted to the Muscovy Company an exclusive monopoly of the Greenland, meaning thereby the Spitzbergen, whale fishery. He claimed these northern waters as the property of the British Crown, because, so it was averred, Hugh Willoughby had in 1553 discovered Spitzbergen. The conferring of this monopoly caused in 1613 a numerous fishing fleet, some of the vessels strongly armed, to set sail from England for Spitzbergen. A landing was made, and the whole archipelago formally annexed and named King James' Newland. The next step of the Muscovy Company's fleet was to clear the ground of intruders, whether foreigners or English 'interlopers.' Among the foreigners were several Dutch boats. These were attacked, boarded, plundered, and then sent home.

Such an act of violence naturally aroused resentment in Holland. The States-General took the matter up, and refused to admit the right of James to interfere with the fishermen. They denied that Hugh Willoughby had sighted Spitzbergen at all in 1553, and confidently affirmed that the discovery of the island was made by Jacob van Heemskerk in 1596, who named it Spitzbergen, planted the Dutch flag upon it, and spent the winter on its shores. If, then, any people had preferential rights in the waters surrounding Spitzbergen, it was the Dutch, but the States did not claim or admit any such rights. They held that the sea was open to all to navigate and to fish in without let or hindrance. To Winwood, who in August, 1613, quitted the Hague to become Secretary of State in London, was entrusted the mission of bringing the complaints and the protest of the States to the notice of James, and further, of asking for reparation to the Amsterdammers, whose vessels had been seized and plundered. The King at this time was anxious to be on friendly terms with the Dutch, and an answer was returned (October 25) that 'not only reparation should be made, but that steps should be taken to prevent a recurrence of such disorders.' The States were not satisfied, however, with so general a reply, and wished that the English claim to exclusive rights in the fisheries should be abandoned. The ambassador Caron was instructed to present to the King an argument from the pen of the geographer Plancius, in which this claim was shown to be without foundation. It produced no effect upon James, always unwilling to yield in a matter affecting his sovereign prerogatives, however shadowy. But the States were equally determined. Their reply to the *non-possumus* attitude of the King was the granting of a charter, early in 1614 (January 27), to a company, generally known as the Northern (sometimes as the Greenland) Company, which conferred on a group of merchants the exclusive privilege of fishing for whales and walrus, and of trading and exploring in the Northern seas between the limits of Nova Zembla and Davis's Straits; Spitzbergen, Bear Island, and Greenland therein included.[27] The States-General likewise consented that warships at the charges of the company should be allowed to accompany the fishing fleet for their protection (April 4). The effect of these strong measures was seen in the changed attitude of the Muscovy Company, who in the summer of 1614 (July 2) made an agreement with their rivals, that they should each of them use a portion of the island as a basis for their fishery, and should unite in keeping out all intruders. The extraordinary mission of Sir Henry Wotton in February, 1615, to the Hague to treat for a settlement of the Jülich-Cleves question, gave an opportunity for proposing that he should, while in the Netherlands, meet Commissioners of the States to discuss also other important matters, and among these the dispute about the so-called 'Greenland' fisheries. In April the conference took place. The Dutch, while laying stress upon their primary rights as discoverers, disclaimed any desire to exclude the English; on the contrary, they endeavoured to arrive at a friendly arrangement by which the two nations should share the fishery 'in unity and security' together. Nothing, however, was effected. The language of King James in his ambassador's instructions, in which mention is made of the differences that had arisen 'on account of the fishery in the North Sea, near the shores of Greenland, of right solely belonging to us and our people, but interrupted by the Hollanders', showed that he approached the subject in an irreconcilable spirit. All that Wotton could say was that he would report the matter to the King, who would inform Caron later of his decision. The affair was, in other words, hung up, and the dangerous spectacle was again witnessed of two fishing fleets carrying on their trade in close proximity, each under the protection of warships.

The Dutch force in 1615 was, however, far stronger, and no hostilities took place. For the same reason an armed peace was maintained in 1617, but in the following year acts of aggression were committed, and loud complaints were raised on both sides. An attempt was now made by the King to strengthen the hands of the Muscovy Company by sanctioning for the purposes of the whale fishery an alliance with the East India Company. The two companies were, as far as regards the Spitzbergen enterprise, to be regarded as one, thus making a larger amount of capital available for the outfit of the fishing fleet and for the maintenance of the storage huts and so-called 'cookeries' on shore. Thirteen well-equipped ships sailed for Spitzbergen in 1618, and an even superior number from Holland and Zeeland, accompanied by two war vessels. Neither the English nor the Dutch sailors were in the mood to brook interference, and from the outset it was almost certain that if they met there would be mischief. The English were the first aggressors, but were in their turn attacked by the Dutch with the result that their fleet was dispersed and many of their vessels plundered. The 'Greenland' fisheries question had reached an acute stage. Such a condition of things could not continue, and Sir Dudley Carleton, the English ambassador, appeared in person before the States-General (October 3, 1618) to utter a strong remonstrance and to urge the States, if they wished to remain on good terms with the King, to dispatch a special embassy to deal with the disputes that had arisen between the two countries, not only concerning the 'Greenland' fishing, but in the East Indies, and about the herring fishery and the cloth trade also.

At this point, before giving an account of the embassy of 1618, we must turn back and bring up to date the history of the herring fishery question from 1610, when the execution of the proclamation requiring a licence from the fishermen was postponed, and also briefly touch upon the two other causes of grievance in regard to the cloth trade and the disputes between the two East India Companies.

For several years after the return of the embassy of 1610 the Dutch herring fishery appears to have been quietly carried on as usual without let or hindrance from the English Government. No attempt was made to enforce the proclamation until 1616. The cause of the alteration of James's policy at that date was due to the refusal of the

States-General to admit English dyed cloths into the United Provinces. The manufacture of woollen cloth had long been the chief of English industries, and the monopoly of the trade in wool and woollen goods in the Netherlands, Northern France and Western Germany had been in the hands of one of the oldest of English Chartered Companies, the Fellowship of Merchant Adventurers[28], whose first charter was granted by Henry VI in 1462. The Adventurer's Court and Staple were for many years placed at Antwerp. But in 1568 they were driven away from the Netherlands by Alva, and forced to settle elsewhere. They went first to Emden, then to Hamburg. But the Hanse towns were jealous of their trade and prosperity, and the Emperor was induced in 1597 to banish them from Germany. At this date the authority of Spain was no longer recognized north of the Scheldt. The Adventurers accordingly in 1598 moved to Middelburg in Zeeland, and extensive privileges were conferred upon them by the States-General, the States of Zeeland, and the town of Middelburg, including freedom from duties on imports or exports, as well as from charges for staple rights and harbour dues, and the right to be tried in their own courts.

The trade of the Adventurers consisted entirely in undyed cloths. The English, though the best weavers of woollen cloth in the world, had not learnt as yet the art of dyeing, and the unfinished cloths were imported into the Netherlands, there to be dressed and dyed for the continental markets. The consequence was that a great industry sprang up in the provinces, especially in Holland, and many thousands of skilled hands were employed in this work.

When James I came to the throne, he listened eagerly to every one who could point out to him any means of raising money by the sale of monopolies or patents. Among the proposals that attracted him was one made by Alderman Sir William Cockayne, who represented to his Majesty the great profit which might be derived from finishing and dyeing English cloth before exportation. The Merchant Adventurers naturally used their utmost influence on the one hand to persuade the King not to grant to Cockayne a patent, which would be subversive of the rights granted to their Company under their Charter, and on the other to obtain the help of the States in preventing such a breach of existing privilege to the injury of the Dutch dyers and finishers. The monopoly of the Adventurers had, however, many enemies among the English merchants who did not belong to the Fellowship, and who already, under the name of 'Interlopers'[29], carried on an extensive illegitimate trade through the ports of Amsterdam and Flushing. Cockayne and his adherents prevailed. A patent was granted to him in 1608, his Majesty reserving to himself the monopoly of the sale of all home-dyed goods. It was clear, however, that the existence of the two monopolies side by side could not continue. After much friction and constant complaints, James, in 1615, took decisive action. He forbade the export of undyed and unfinished cloth from England, and commanded the Merchant Adventurers to return their Charter. Cockayne immediately formed a company, but his hopes of creating a new and lucrative English industry were speedily dashed to the ground. The States of Holland passed a resolution forbidding the importation of dyed cloths into their province, and their example was followed by the other provinces separately, and by the States-General. The English woollen trade was stricken fatally by such a prohibition, Cockayne's Company failed, and James was at last compelled in 1617 to renew the Charter of the Adventurers.

It is needless to say that the King, who had hoped to replenish his empty treasury through his active promotion of Cockayne's scheme, was sorely disappointed at the issue, and deeply resented the strong measures taken by Holland and the United Provinces generally to checkmate his plan for the creation of a new English industry to their injury. Baulked in this direction, James, on his side, turned his thoughts to reprisals, and in so doing had on this occasion the full approval of his subjects. Secretary Winwood wrote, September 14, 1616, to Sir Dudley Carleton, at the Hague:—

'It is in the mouth of every true-hearted Englishman that as a reprisal for the publication of the rigorous placard against English dyed and dressed cloths, that his Majesty with justice and equity and in reason of state ought to forbid the Hollanders, by a fresh revival of former proclamations, to continue their yearly fishing on our coast.'

But Winwood had had long personal knowledge of the Dutch, and he did not like the prospect of the two nations, so long and closely bound together by ties of friendship and alliance, thus drifting apart through trade rivalries into enmity.

'If we come', he writes, 'to these extremities I know both we and they shall suffer and smart for it'. And then he continues in words rendered weighty by the experience which lay behind them: 'I know well the nature of that people and the humour of those masters, who sit at the stern of that State. They will not be willingly crossed in their courses—*et quod volunt, valde volunt*. Yet it is never too late to be wise, and no counsel is evil but that which cannot be changed. I profess unto you I am in great anguish of spirit, how to accommodate these differences to the full contentment of all parties. This is most certain—*couste que couste*—and though *coelum terris misceatur*, his Majesty is resolved not to swallow, much less to digest, these indignities. As before I have said, only the Spaniards have cause to triumph and to make bonfires of joy and gladness.' He requests Carleton to see Oldenbarneveldt and urge accommodation for the mutual good of both countries. 'If the States', he adds, 'do persist in their resolutions, *actum est de amicitia*.'[50]

But although Winwood speaks in this letter, dated September 24, as if the King was only considering the question of a revival of the proclamation of 1609, steps had already been taken (apparently with his knowledge) to levy a toll upon the fishers on the Scottish coast. As early as June 16, the Duke of Lennox, in his capacity as Admiral of Scotland, had received instructions from the Scottish Council to take from every fishing 'buss' a payment either in money (an angelot) or in kind (one ton of herring and twelve codfish). Accordingly, on August 7, a vessel appeared in the midst of the fishing fleet, having on board a certain John Browne, the Duke's Secretary. The Dutch envoy (Caron) had been induced, under a misconception of the purpose for which it was required, to write a commendatory letter for this man to show to the captains of the Dutch convoy-ships. Browne demanded in the name of the King from the skippers of each 'buss' the above-named toll or excise, and he proceeded to make a list of all their names and the names of the boats, giving receipts to those who paid, and informing those who did not do so that they would have to pay double the following year. The greater part paid without opposition, until the two convoy-ships arrived on the scene. Browne was seized and requested to produce his commission. At the sight of Caron's letter, however, they dismissed him, as he had used no violence, but they would not allow him to collect any more toll.

The two captains, as in duty bound, reported the matter at once to the home authorities. Great was the surprise and indignation at Enkhuysen and other centres of the fishing industry at the reception of the news. On August 27 it was discussed by the States-General, who denounced the attempt to levy a toll as 'an unheard-of and unendurable novelty, conflicting with previous treaties'. Two dispatches were sent, one to Caron telling him 'that the States had taken the matter extremely to heart, and desired him to seek for redress by every possible means'; the other to the captains of the convoy bidding them 'not to permit any toll to be exacted'. In obedience to his instructions Caron made repeated representations to the King, to Lennox, to the Scottish Council, but his arguments and remonstrances fell on deaf ears, and his efforts to obtain satisfaction proved fruitless. In these circumstances the opening of the fishing season of 1617 was awaited in Holland with anxiety, and by those acquainted with the temper of the Dutch seamen, with apprehension. Their fears were justified.

Browne again visited the fishing fleet, and began his task of levying toll, which according to all testimony he carried out in a tactful and considerate manner. Arriving at the Rotterdam convoy-ship he met with a flat refusal from the captain, Andries Tlieff of Rotterdam, in his own name and that of the other Dutch fishermen. After having received this refusal in writing, Browne was preparing quietly to go away to visit the other fishing boats, mostly French, when Jan Albertsz, captain of the Enkhuysen convoy-ship, stepped on board. He was one of the two captains who had in the previous year forcibly compelled Browne to stop his collection of toll. Albertsz now declared that he had orders to arrest Browne, and, despite his protests, the Scottish official was made a prisoner and carried to Holland.

The indignation of James, when he heard of what had taken place, knew no bounds. Two captains of Dutch vessels in the Thames were seized, as hostages, and Carleton was instructed to go in person to the States-General and demand satisfaction for the insult and injury done to his Majesty's honour by the 'exemplary punishment and in a public and open fashion of those, who had committed such an act: a satisfaction such as may hold a just proportion unto the insolency of the grievance.'[31] On August 23, Carleton, describing the result of an interview with the Advocate, spoke of 'Barneveldt not knowing what to say, but that the taking of Browne was ill-done, and desiring me with his hat in his hand (much differing from his use) to make report thereof to his Majesty.' Both he and also Maurice disavowed Albertsz's action, and the States-General in their turn declared that the captains had acted without instructions, and ordered Browne to be released. At the same time they respectfully insisted that their fishermen were specially exempted from paying any toll for their fishing. They ask Carleton to beg James, as Browne had been set free, to release the hostages that he had seized. But Winwood peremptorily informed Carleton (August 27, O.S.), 'His Majesty will take no satisfaction, but to have the captains and chief officers of the ships sent over prisoners to England.' This demand, however, was most unpalatable in Holland. The States of that province stood upon their privileges. The captains should be tried, they said, but only by their own courts and laws. James, however, would not give way. In Winwood's words 'he insisted, *fort et ferme*, on the offenders being delivered into his hands'. Thus for many months the obstinate dispute continued. At last (February 1) the States of Holland, the opposition of the towns of Rotterdam and Enkhuysen to deliver up their citizens having been overcome, consented that Albertsz and Tlieff should be sent to Noel Caron to submit themselves to his Majesty's mercy, 'for which,' says Carleton,₍₂₃₎ 'in a letter they sue, and' he adds 'they also ask for the freedom of fishing on the coast of Scotland, to which they lay claim, without molestation.' Not till April did Tlieff actually set sail for England, and then without the worse offender, Albertsz, who was very ill, and in fact died shortly afterwards. James now, however, professed himself satisfied, the hostages were set free, and the Browne incident closed without a breach of the peace.

The fishery dispute meanwhile remained an open sore. Loud complaints were made by the Scottish Council that the Dutch not only claimed the right to fish free from any toll, but they under the protection of their armed convoy hindered the Scottish boats from fishing, and took away their nets and otherwise treated them 'with daily outrages and insolences'. This was the state of affairs in 1617. Carleton made many and strong remonstrances, but in 1618 the complaints of the Scotch that they were driven away from the fishing grounds by acts of violence were louder than ever. Instructions had been given to Carleton (April 10, 1618) that, as a means for avoiding these disputes and encounters, he should request the States to order their fishermen to ply their trade out of sight of land, as had been, so he averred, their former custom. After a delay of two months the States, while promising to punish severely all who could be shown to have committed such acts as those complained of, declared that after examination of witnesses on oath they could not discover that any offences such as those spoken of by the King had taken place. As to the Netherlanders fishing out of sight of land, they denied any knowledge of such a custom, and prayed the King not to disturb their countrymen in the exercise of that right of free fishing granted them from time immemorial by a succession of treaties.

Thus in the summer of 1618 we have seen that no less than three burning questions—the Greenland or Spitzbergen fishery, the Great or Herring fishery, and the refusal to admit English dyed or dressed cloths into the Netherlands—were causing the relations between England and the United Provinces to be very strained. A fourth question, that of the disputes of the rival East India Companies as to trading rights in the Banda Islands, Amboyna, and the Moluccas, where the Dutch, being in far stronger force, prevented the English from sharing in the lucrative commerce in spices, was also becoming acute. Several islands—among them one named Pulo Run, which the English, by the consent of the natives, had occupied—were seized by the Dutch, and actual hostilities between the fleets representing the two nations in those waters were only avoided because the English were not in a position to offer effective resistance to their superior adversaries. Negotiations had therefore been set on foot as early as 1615 to effect a friendly understanding by which the English should be allowed a fair share in the spice trade, and the companies co-operate for their common interest. So far, however, in 1618, were matters from being arranged, that a strong fleet had been dispatched from London in that year under Sir Thomas Dale to restore the balance of power in the Bunda archipelago.

When, therefore, as has been already related, Carleton on October 3 appeared in the States-General to protest in the strongest possible language against the acts of hostility committed against the fishing fleet of the Muscovy Company off Spitzbergen, he did not confine himself to this one cause of embittered dispute, but demanded that the States should send at once, promptly and without delay, the special embassy, which had been often spoken of but never taken seriously in hand, to discuss in London all the points of difference between the two nations—the East Indian spice trade, the herring fishery, and the dyed cloth question—and to strive to arrive at a friendly arrangement. Otherwise, he warned them that the King, though he had shown himself willing to bear much at their hands, had now reached the limit of his endurance.

III: 1618-1623

In the Netherlands the minds of all men were throughout the year 1618 preoccupied with the fierce political and religious discords that had brought civil strife into the land. The sword of Maurice had, in the name of the States-General of the Union, overthrown the power of the provincial oligarchies, and despite the strenuous opposition of the States of Holland under the leadership of Oldenbarneveldt, had made good the claim of the States-General to sovereign authority in the Republic. The aged Advocate of Holland, so long supreme in the administration of public affairs, with his chief adherents, lay in prison awaiting trial and condemnation. Anxious, therefore, at such a crisis, to avoid a breach with King James, or to provoke on his part measures of reprisal (especially in view of the approaching meeting of the Synod of Dort, at which James was to be officially represented), the States announced their readiness (October 18) to accede to Carleton's request for the speedy dispatch of a special embassy. But they wished to confine the subjects of discussion to the East Indian and Greenland disputes. In vain Carleton pressed upon the States the urgency of including the Great (Herring) Fishery and dyed cloth questions in the instruction. The reply was that it would be dangerous in the disturbed condition of the country to touch matters of such great importance affecting the interests of so large a portion of the population of the maritime provinces. A clear indication was moreover given that on these two points there was little possibility of concession.

The ambassadors arrived in England (December 7) accompanied by five commissioners of the East India Company. The King received them with expressions of friendliness (December 20), but the examination of their instructions by the Privy Council at once revealed that the subject of the Great Fisheries, which had most interest for the English, was omitted. The Dutch envoys accordingly were informed that the King was very astonished that the warnings of Carleton had been without effect, and that their mission would be fruitless unless this point, which concerned the King's sovereign rights, were placed in the forefront of the negotiations. James, indeed, refused to proceed unless the instructions were altered, and held out the threat of an alliance with Spain if his wishes were not complied with. Carleton, indeed, in a long and angry representation made to the States-General, January 12, 1619, practically demanded, not only that the ambassadors should be instructed to deal with the Great Fishery question, but to admit that their rights under ancient treaties and their contention as to the freedom of the sea were claims that could not be sustained in face of the King's 'lawful title and exclusive sovereign rights and property in the fisheries upon the coasts of his three kingdoms'. In case of delay, England would maintain her rights with the armed hand. The King was resolved that the grievances of which his subjects complained must cease.

The States-General, however, dared not in the midst of the crisis through which the country was passing, interfere with the fishery question. Maurice, as Captain-General of the Union, had by military force overpowered the resistance of the Province of Holland to the will of the States-General. Its leaders had been incarcerated, and the town magistracies throughout Holland changed. Feelings were very embittered, and the position of the new magistrates would have been seriously endangered had the dominant party consented to yield to English threats the rights of free fishing, an industry on which some 50,000 persons in Holland depended for their livelihood. Both Maurice and his cousin and trusted adviser, William Lewis of Nassau, Stadholder of Friesland, were agreed that such a course was at the moment unwise, if not impracticable. These considerations were laid before James, who had throughout the discussions in the Republic strongly sympathized with the triumphant Contra-Remonstrant party. The result was a modification in his unbending attitude. The King agreed to defer the discussion of the 'Great Fishery' question until the internal state of the Netherlands had become more settled, and to proceed with the Greenland fishery and East Indian matters first, on condition that the delay was to be as short as possible and not to extend beyond the end of the year. Indeed, September 1 was named as the actual limit of time. The States were quickly informed (January 21) of the English concession, and now that the tension was relieved, took more than three weeks in which to consider carefully the terms of their answer to Carleton. They were in a difficult position, and they finally (February 13) gave in general terms a non-committal undertaking that 'so soon as the affairs of this land, political and religious, shall be brought into a better state—if possible within a year', they will send ambassadors to treat of the Great Fishery, the cloth trade, and other points, as a preliminary to the revision of the treaties of intercourse. Meanwhile they trusted that all should go on as before, and that the English would make no innovation in contravention of the ancient customs and treaties. So the matter rested, the States being warned that the King demanded that the placard of June 5, 1618, forbidding the Dutch fishermen to commit further outrages and excesses 'on pain of severe penalties', or to approach within sight (the English said within 14 miles, but to this the Dutch objected) of the Scottish coast, should be rigidly enforced during the intermediate period of delay.

The efforts of the Dutch ambassadors to settle the two questions which according to their instructions were the chief object of their mission nevertheless encountered serious difficulties, and it was soon apparent that the views of the two parties were almost irreconcilable. The scheme for a working union of the two East India Companies was speedily given up. For months, however, the rights and wrongs of the two nations with regard to the Greenland (Spitzbergen) fisheries were the subject of many conferences and interchanges of notes. The English maintained that they, on the ground of first discovery and of being the first to fish in the Spitzbergen waters, had exclusive rights of sovereignty both on the land and the seas that surrounded it. The Dutch set up the counter-claim that they had not only first discovered, but first occupied the land, and they held firmly that the sea was free to all nations. For the damages suffered by the English fishing fleet at the hands of the Netherlanders in 1618 an indemnity was demanded by the English Government amounting to £43,800, and this did not include the amounts due to private ship-owners for the loss of their trade, and to the relatives of those who had been killed or wounded. The Dutch replied by pointing to the repeated provocations the Hollanders and Zeelanders had had year by year to endure, and to the losses they on their side had suffered not only through being hindered in their fishing, but through actual plundering of their goods. The ambassadors promised to give reparation, if the English would do the same. Tired at last of fruitless discussions, prolonged month after month, the Dutch envoys sought a personal interview with the King, July 10, at Greenwich, to see if any *modus vivendi* could be arrived at. All the old arguments on both sides were repeated, and neither would yield on the point of their several 'rights'; the utmost the King would concede was a suggestion that, as a favour, he might connive at the Netherlanders fishing in his waters. This did not satisfy the ambassadors, and they fell back on the familiar device of asking that the question should be put off for later settlement. To this finally James agreed, and it was arranged that the matter should be deferred for further negotiations for a period of three years, and that meanwhile the English and Dutch were to fish peaceably together. The King insisted that restitution should be made for the damage done by the armed attack on the English fleet in 1618 within three months, and for all other losses inflicted by the Dutch within the three years. As soon as the full English claims were settled (such was the ultimatum), the question of the satisfaction due to the Netherlanders should be considered. With this decision, however unpalatable to them, the envoys had perforce to be content. They sailed from Gravesend, on August 1, without having really effected anything but a postponement of disputes, which mere delay was more likely to aggravate than to appease.

The results then of the embassy of 1618 were disappointing to both parties. The English resented the continued presence of the Dutch fishermen both in the home waters and in the Northern Seas, for they not only carried off the profits from what were regarded as British industries, but behaved with overbearing arrogance as if in their own domain. The Hollanders found themselves permitted, as it were on sufferance, to continue an occupation which supplied a large part of their population with sustenance and was the basis of their prosperity. The States-General, though they were committed by their envoys to send a fresh embassy to deal with the question of the Great Fisheries, as soon as the internal troubles of the country were settled, were in no hurry to move in the matter. It was in vain that Carleton in the early months of 1620 reminded them of their undertaking. The general opinion in Holland, and in this Prince Maurice himself shared, was that there could be no surrender of the treaty right to free fishing, even though it should be at the cost of war.

Their position was greatly strengthened by the momentous events that had been occurring in Germany. The Elector Palatine, Frederick—King James's son-in-law—had accepted the Crown of Bohemia (November, 1619) but a year later his forces were crushed by the Imperial army at the White Hill near Prague (November 5). Meanwhile his hereditary dominions had been invaded and conquered by a Spanish force under Spinola. Frederick was head of the Protestant Union, but the forces of the Union were disunited (indeed it was soon afterwards dissolved), and although Sir Horace Vere, at the head of a fine body of 2,000 English volunteers, escorted by a strong Dutch force, made his way to the scene of conflict, he was unable to prevent the Spanish conquest of the Lower Palatinate. The unfortunate King of Bohemia, a homeless fugitive, was compelled with his wife, Elizabeth of England, to seek refuge with his uncle, the Prince of Orange, at the Hague. The Dutch were greatly disturbed, as the twelve years' truce was drawing to an end, at the prospect of the Spaniards being able through their alliance with the Emperor to march from their post of vantage on the Rhine straight upon the Netherlands, and were therefore anxious to secure the goodwill and help of England in the serious struggle which they saw before them. They felt confident that, despite his love of peace, James would be forced to take active steps to defend his son-in-law's lands from conquest, and the cause of Protestantism in Germany from ruin. The news of the complete defeat of Frederick at the White Hill therefore, together with the necessity of renewing the treaty between the two countries, which expired in April, 1621, at the end of the truce, had more effect than Carleton's remonstrances and threats in hastening a renewal of negotiations. The English ambassador was instructed to assure the States that James would lend assistance for the recovery of the Palatinate, and it was resolved by them that a special mission should be dispatched as soon as possible. It was well known that the King was still on the most confidential terms with Gondomar, and that the Spanish envoy continued to exercise a strong influence upon the royal policy, and that the project of a Spanish marriage had not been abandoned. It was felt therefore that a strong effort should be made to counteract this secret leaning of James to listen to the subtle counsels of the Spaniard, and to persuade him to break with Spain and to take decisively the Protestant side in the war against the allied forces of the House of Habsburg.

The ambassadors set sail from Veere, January 28, 1621, and arrived in London on February 1. They were six in number, representing the three maritime provinces of Holland, Zeeland, and Friesland, in itself a proof that though the affairs of the Palatinate were the principal subject that filled their instructions, the fishery questions, for the moment placed in the background, had in reality lost none of their importance. The names of the special envoys were Jonkheer Jacobus van Wijngaerden, Johan Camerling, Albert Sonck, Albert Bruyninck, Jacobus Schotte, and Jonkheer Frederik van Vervou tot Martenahuys, and with them was associated the resident in London, Noel Caron. At their first audience with the King (February 7) the situation in Germany was almost exclusively referred to. They laid stress upon the extent of the

Spanish conquests on the Rhine, and after pointing out that the States had been paying monthly subsidies to certain of the Protestant princes and had collected a great army on the frontier, expressed their gratification at the information that had been received through Sir Dudley Carleton to the effect that the King would, if diplomacy failed, restore his children in the possessions by force. Should he indeed be prepared to take steps for military intervention, they were commissioned to assure him that the States would be ready to second his action and to go to war.

The embassy had arrived at a critical moment in the reign of James I, and after some words of friendly compliment their conference with the Privy Council was deferred until February 15. In the interval James's third Parliament had met (February 9). The King's financial necessities had forced him to summon a Parliament, and the session was to prove a very stormy one. The leaders of the Commons at once demanded the redress of many grievances and proceeded to attack those whom they charged with being the cause of the abuses they denounced, more especially the omnipotent favourite, Buckingham himself. The sojourn of the Dutch mission therefore coincided with a period of political stress and anxiety. But the envoys had the satisfaction of knowing that the English Parliament, which in this was thoroughly representative of public opinion in the country, was enthusiastically in favour of active support being given to the King of Bohemia for the recovery of the Palatinate. Subsidies were without delay voted for that purpose, and the vote was accompanied by a petition urging the King to make war with Spain and to break off the negotiations for the Spanish marriage.

But Gondomar found no difficulty in trading upon James's habitual preference for peaceful methods. According to the testimony of the Venetian, Girolamo Lando, the Spanish ambassador 'had access to the King at any hour, and found all doors open to him which were accustomed to be shut to others', and he is described as 'with ever-increasing boldness carrying on a campaign against these kingdoms with unspeakable intrigues and corruption.' Through his counsels the King entered upon a series of negotiations with the Courts of Madrid and Vienna in the interests of Frederick, which were perfectly futile and merely afforded the Catholic powers time to strengthen their position upon the Rhine. At the same time James, by opposing himself to the expressed wishes of his Parliament and people in this matter of the Palatinate, only heightened the determination of the House of Commons to assert their privileges and insist upon their demand for a redress of grievances. In foreign no less than in domestic affairs, the views of the King and those of the representatives of his people proved to be diametrically opposed. In December accordingly, no compromise being possible, Parliament was dissolved, and James, left in desperate financial straits, was unable to carry out any policy that involved expenditure. In considering the course of the negotiations with the Dutch, these facts must be borne in mind, for they are vitally important for a right understanding of the situation.

The embassy, delayed by the opening of Parliament, had a conference with the Privy Council on February 15. Once more they impressed upon their audience the seriousness of the dangers which threatened both the United Provinces and England from the war in Germany, and urged, now that the truce with Spain was almost expired, the renewal of the treaty of alliance between the two countries to defend the Protestant cause against a common enemy. In the words of the contemporary historian Aitzema, 'they laid strong emphasis upon this last point as if it were the only object and aim of the embassy.' But the Council had no desire, so immediately after the meeting of Parliament, to commit themselves on the subject of military intervention, for they were well aware of the King's disinclination to break with Spain. The question was accordingly put to the Dutchmen as to whether there were no other points in their instructions, mention being specially made of the fisheries, the cloth, and the East Indian disputes. The reply was that in the present critical condition of European affairs the interest of both States required that secondary questions should be allowed to rest and continue on the same footing as before in the presence of the grave danger (now the truce was drawing to an end) from a mighty enemy. Some lesser differences which had arisen about the 'tare' in the cloth trade, and the 'mint', they were ready to discuss, but nothing more.

The matter was referred to the King, and on March 2 the envoys had a second conference with the Council, when it was made clear to them that the fisheries questions must be settled as a preliminary to any treaty of alliance. The Dutch could only answer (March 10) that they had received no powers to negotiate upon the fisheries, but in accordance with their instructions they pointed out the difficulty and the danger of trying to interfere with an industry in which so large a part of the population were interested, while civil discords were scarcely appeased and a renewal of the war with Spain was on the point of breaking out. So much was this the case that though the value of the fishing (so they said) was steadily decreasing, the States were granting large subsidies for convoys in order to provide the means of sustenance for so large a number of their subjects. The smallest toll or charge, they argued, would either cause 'their fishery to be entirely destroyed and ruined, or possibly stir up this rude sea-faring population to fresh commotions to the manifest peril of the repose of the Republic, scarcely cured of the wounds of its late infirmity.' They begged therefore that the consideration of the matter might be put off to a more fitting time, and meanwhile that the old privileges should continue in force. As to the Greenland fishery, it was pleaded that the three years' delay that had been granted in 1619 was not yet expired. Similarly in the East Indian disputes, which continued with no less frequency and bitterness, although an accord between the two companies had been agreed upon in June, 1619, the Netherlanders met the complaints of the representatives of the English Company with excuses and counter-protests. There was much talking, but practically no progress made. After several interviews with the Council and the King himself it was finally arranged that things should remain as they were for a short time longer, but the King insisted (April 8) that 'the fishery questions concerned his right and his honour and that he could not allow them to be any longer in debate and suspense', and that a special Commission must be sent by the States to deal with these disputes, and further, that he would not wait longer than May 31. He also demanded a settlement of the quarrels in the East Indies, and a withdrawal of the 'tare' edict, which was declared to be the ruin of the cloth industry in England. So soon as these matters were satisfactorily arranged, he promised that he would conclude an alliance with the States. The Dutch envoys left London on their return journey on April 26.

As a proof of the very close relations subsisting at this time between England and the United Provinces, it may be mentioned that in the very same months that the Wijngaerden embassy was thus holding ineffectual conferences in London with the King of England and his Privy Council, the Fellowship of the Merchant Adventurers were transferring their Court to the Prinsenhof at Delft.

Driven from Antwerp in 1582 the Adventurers had, as already related, set up their Great Court first at Emden, then at Hamburg and Stade. But in 1598 the enmity of the Hanse towns compelled them to leave Stade, and to establish themselves at Middelburg in Zeeland. Until the suppression of the Adventurers' Charter in 1615, this town was the staple for English cloth and wool in the Netherlands, though the 'interlopers' as they were called, succeeded in carrying on an active smuggling trade through Amsterdam and Flushing. After the renewal of the Charter in 1617 the Adventurers returned to Middelburg, but on account of the unhealthiness of the place, and other reasons, they determined to remove to Delft. To effect this involved elaborate negotiations with the Town Corporation, with the States of Holland, and with the States-General. Moreover, the consent of the King was necessary as a preliminary step. Sir Dudley Carleton was largely instrumental in bringing the matter to a successful issue. James gave his consent that the Court should move from Zeeland within the borders of Holland, 'to show his Majesty's great affection for that Province'. On April 21, 1621, the contract with Delft was signed, just as the Dutch envoys were leaving England. But Amsterdam, with whose cloth merchants the 'interlopers' had been engaged in a profitable trade, sent in to the States of Holland a very strongly worded remonstrance. They objected to the privileges which the Delft Corporation had granted to the Adventurers as injurious to themselves and the interests of the province. The States of Holland on receiving this remonstrance resolved that the contract made by Delft and the monopoly of the Adventurers should be examined by a commission. Against this Delft and a number of other towns sent in a counter-remonstrance, but the influence of Amsterdam outweighed theirs in the provincial States, who by a majority of votes persisted in their determination. The Merchant Adventurers, however, appealed from the provincial authorities to the States-General, who had always been their protectors. And now began one of those curious struggles so common in Dutch history between the town of Delft, the States of Holland, and the States-General, all of them claiming independent authority to deal with the matter. The Corporation of Delft refused to hand over their contract with the Merchant Adventurers to be examined by the Commission of the States of Holland. At last, however, it was agreed by both parties that it should be placed in the hands of Prince Maurice and some impartial persons, who should then confer with the States, and draw 'a good regulation for the preserving of the common industries'. Maurice appointed a commission on which the ten towns interested in the cloth trade (of which naturally Delft was one) were represented, to take the matter in hand, and on June 19, 1621, the 'Regulation' was drawn up which defined the privileges and conditions under which the Adventurers henceforth for many years carried on their trade in Holland. Its terms therefore deserve to be briefly indicated. The old privileges giving freedom from import and export duties, harbour and market tolls, &c., originally granted in 1598, were not revoked, but defined afresh and modified. Art. i gave the Fellowship permission to have their Court at Delft, but only with the licences 'which we [the States of Holland] and the States-General shall be pleased to accord, in trust that the Netherlanders shall enjoy their old privileges in England.' This last clause clearly referred to the fishing rights, with which at that very moment the English Government were proposing to interfere. Art. ii reminded the Adventurers that when residing in Holland 'they would be subject to all our edicts and enactments made or still to make.' Art. iii dealt with the excise recently imposed on foreign woollen cloth. On this no concession was made; it must be promptly paid. Art. iv insisted on the strict carrying out of the edict of 1614 forbidding the importation of dyed or prepared cloth, and also of the edict on the 'tare', which had been renewed in 1617. Both these edicts were regarded as grievances by the English, and had in 1618 and in 1621 been among the subjects on which negotiations had proved fruitless.

Before this 'Regulation' of June 19, 1621, had come into force the time fixed by King James for the dispatch of another embassy to settle all outstanding disputes had passed by. Through the representations of Carleton at the Hague, and the letters of their own ambassador Caron from London, it was made clear, however, to the States that a temporizing policy was no longer possible. Indefinite delay would not be brooked. Steps were accordingly taken to approach certain of those who claimed damages against the Greenland Company with an offer to compound with them by a cash payment. Nor did the States confine themselves to words, but gave practical proof of their desire for peace, for when the Greenland Company applied for a convoy of warships to accompany the whale-fishing fleet to Spitzbergen, the States-General, after consultation with the States of Holland, declined to grant the request, April 28. The determined attitude of Carleton, who threatened reprisals in the Channel upon the ships returning from the East Indies had its effect, and the slow-moving Netherlanders were at last stirred to action. The new envoys were appointed early in October, and though even after their nomination there was further delay while the instructions were being drawn up, within two months all preliminaries were completed, and the embassy finally arrived in London, December 8, 1621.

Its arrival coincided with the final rupture between James and his Parliament, and the situation was far from favourable to a really friendly settlement. The King was in bad health, worried and embittered in temper by the affronts which he had just been enduring from what he regarded as the insolent demands of a House of Commons which neither by threats nor by persuasion had he been able to bend to his will. Both Philip III of Spain and the Archduke Albert of the Netherlands had recently died. A young king reigned in Madrid, but his favourite, the Count of Olivares, held the reins of power, a man filled with the ambition of raising Spain once again to her old position of ascendancy in Europe. His policy, as stated in the Cortes of Castile, was to assist the Emperor to crush the Protestant cause in Bohemia and in Germany, to attack the Dutch rebels now that the truce was expired, and to defend with all the power of the monarchy 'the sacred Catholic faith and the authority of the Holy See'. Yet in spite of so clear a declaration James fell more and more under the spell exercised over him by Gondomar, who had Buckingham and other English councillors in his pay, and who continued to dangle before the eyes of the infatuated King, still dreaming of a Spanish match for his son, the hope that by the friendly intervention of Philip IV at Vienna, he might be able to secure without hostilities good terms for his son-in-law, and a settlement of the Dutch and other questions in a manner satisfactory to all parties. It was, of course, a purely visionary project, nevertheless it is probable that James was sincere in his aims, and thought that he was acting nobly in playing the part of arbiter of peace and war. But he was really a puppet in the hands of those who were far more astute than himself, and who, while he was negotiating, were grimly preparing for the prosecution in real earnest of the longest and most cruel war Europe has ever seen. It was well known moreover to the statesmen, who treated him as their dupe, that the breach between James and his Parliament effectually prevented him, even if he wished it, from serious intervention.

The Dutch Embassy, which was accompanied by three Commissioners on behalf of the East India Company, had at its head Francis van Aerssen, Lord of Sommelsdijk. Aerssen, already distinguished as a diplomatist and noted for the prominent part he had taken in the recent overthrow of Oldenbarneveldt, was for many years to be the trusted councillor of the Stadholders Maurice and Frederick Henry. Richelieu, at a later time, spoke of him as one of the three ablest statesmen of his time. He had now before him a long and difficult task. Aitzema lays special emphasis on the duration and the expense of this special mission. It lasted, he tells us, 454 days, and cost 80,850 guilders. 'In the course of it', he further remarks, 'King James at the audiences made very particular and most remarkable discourses, which were replied to by the Lord of Sommelsdijk with exceptional prudence, he being a man of great sharp-sightedness, eloquence, and experience.'

xl

The skill of Aerssen is shown in the instructions for the embassy, which, once more according to Aitzema, were drawn up by himself. The following are the important points. Art. vii deals with the 'questions which have arisen on the whale fishery between the English nation and the Greenland Company of their lands and their differences concerning the pretended losses suffered on either side.' The envoys are instructed, if possible, to come to a friendly understanding, 'if not, by authoritative decision to draw up for the future a Regulation of the aforesaid fishery' on the lines of the previous negotiations, but 'not so as to cause any disadvantage to the land's service or to the rights of the privileged company,' Above all, nothing is to be concluded on this matter without awaiting the orders of the States-General, should time and opportunity permit. The next five articles treat of the affairs of the two East India Companies, which were, in fact, the main object of the mission. The cloth trade disputes are next dealt with. If complaints should be made about the raising by the States of Holland of the duty on foreign woollen goods, the lines of defence are laid down in Arts. xiv and xv. In Art. xvi the envoys are bidden to avoid any reopening of the 'tare' question, but should the placard enforcing an examination of the goods by the tare-masters be denounced, it must be shown to be necessary in the interests of the cloth trade, and for the prevention of fraud. If English subjects pretend to suffer any injury through the 'tare', let them bring their grievances before their High Mightinesses, who will see that justice is done. Likewise on the subject of the 'interlopers' (Art. xvii) silence is enjoined. The reply, however, to any complaint is that his Majesty has the remedy in his own hands by forbidding the 'interlopers' to trade. It would be far easier to prevent their egress from England than their ingress into the United Provinces. Art. xviii deals with the question of the Mint. Last of all, the instructions arrive at the Great Fisheries difficulty. The envoys are carefully to avoid any reference to this matter. If compelled to speak about it, they are to say that they have received no instructions thereon,

'as their High Mightinesses had hoped that the King would leave this matter untouched, as His Majesty had thought good to delay this whole question for a further period still and a more fitting season. In any case this industry is necessary for the subsistence of many thousands of the sea-faring folk of their Lands, and to consent to a course that would ruin them is *impossible*, and there is no hope that such consent would be given either now or hereafter.'

Conferences were held with the Privy Council on January 15, February 17, and March 14, the Dutch trying to concentrate attention on the East Indian differences, about which public opinion in England as well as in Holland had been much stirred, and about the renewal of the treaty of alliance, urging that the King should take sides with his old allies against the Spaniards and active steps to recover the Palatinate for his son-in-law. Buckingham's efforts to discuss the alleged acts of violence by the Dutch fishermen to the King's Scottish subjects only led to the reply that the States had issued a strong edict against such acts and would punish them if proved. As no progress to any agreement was being reached, the envoys suggested a personal audience with the King. This was granted on April 27. James was far from well, and in a very irritable humour. He received them alone, and, contrary to his habit, sat in his chair during the interview with his hat on, while the ambassadors stood the whole time with uncovered heads. Aerssen, after the usual compliments, spoke at considerable length, in accordance with the terms of his instructions, upon the East Indian and other matters on which the States desired to treat. The effect of this speech is best told in the words of the original report of the proceedings:—

'They [the envoys] noted that His Majesty was entirely prejudiced and prepared by his Council to set his heart against them. To their compliments he gave no reply, letting them pass unnoticed. When they (through their spokesman Aerssen) were entering into the business, he said, "Make an end of your long harangue. I will give a short and good answer. You are a good orator, I know it well; when I was younger, so was I also; now my memory fails me." Six times with great discourtesy did he interrupt them.'

The violence of the 'short and good answer' in which he finally poured forth the pent-up vials of his wrath upon the Dutchmen is at least a proof that James, despite his age and infirmities, still possessed considerable powers of invective. Speaking of the East Indian disputes, he exclaimed:—

'You have taken away the goods of my subjects, have made war on, murdered and mishandled them, without once thinking of what you have enjoyed from this Crown, which has made you and maintained you. You must give them satisfaction.... I hold that you ought to show respect to my nation. You are speaking of the accord (of 1619), I decline to treat with you on equal terms. You have in the Indies a Man who well deserves to be hanged. Your people over there represent everywhere your Prince of Orange as a great King and Lord, and hold me up as a little kinglet, as if I stood under him, thus misleading the barbarian kings.

Tell me what you are thinking of doing, whether you will take action and give me satisfaction or not? Will you do it, then do it the sooner the better; it will be best for you; when will you begin? Surely you are like leeches, bloodsuckers of my realm, you draw the blood from my subjects and seek to ruin me; there are six points that show it clearly; take *the great fishery*—you come here to land against the will of my subjects, you do them damage, you injure them, you desecrate the Churches, doing filthy acts in them, you hinder them from fishing; the Greenland whale fishery you wish to dispute with me, without making good the loss; France and Spain have ceded it to me, with Denmark I have come to an agreement, you alone wish to maintain it against me. I would not endure it either from France or from Spain, do you think I either can or will bear it from you? In the Cloths you are playing at *passe-passe*, as if you were laying a burden on your inhabitants, and yet this is the cause; these (the Cloths) are no more carried, therefrom as you may have heard a mutiny and wellnigh a rebellion exists in my Realm.'

Having mentioned these three points, the other three appear to have escaped his Majesty's memory. After this outburst the negotiations were renewed, the East Indian questions being taken first. This admirably suited the Dutch, who knew they had the upper hand in the Indies and were anxious to shelve the fishery dispute as long as possible. For months the weary negotiations proceeded, until in August there was once more a deadlock. The King again granted an audience (August 16), was again angry, and with small result. An event now occurred which gave rise to fresh complaint. The Dutch fishermen off the Scottish coast had encountered an Ostend vessel with some Dutch prisoners on board. The Ostender was attacked and an attempt made to set the captives free. A conference was held on the matter in the King's presence, September 25, and the Hollanders were accused of a breach of neutrality. The envoys rejoined that it was the Ostender which had committed a breach of neutrality by bringing prisoners into Scottish waters, and pointed out 'that no one had so great an interest as his Majesty to prevent Spain from sharing the sovereignty of the sea on which his Majesty was so mighty and whereon his chief security lay'. This reference to James's relations with Spain was more than the testy King could brook.

'It is you', he said, 'who are masters of the sea, far and wide, you do just what you like, you hinder my own subjects from fishing on my coasts, who at any rate according to all Rights ought to enjoy the first benefit, but when I raise the question, and urge you to observe my rights, to listen to what I have to say, you will not agree to a single word being spoken about it; yes, my ambassador writes to me that he might just as well speak to you of the rights of my fishery, as of a declaration of war with you. When you are at war, you say that your Government has not yet been granted time for your community to get on its legs. In peace, you have other excuses. The long and the short is, you don't want to enter into it.'

The ambassadors were, however, not to be entrapped into a discussion of the Great Fisheries; remarking that his Majesty had agreed to defer speaking about this question, they skilfully turned his attention to other subjects. One result of this conference was the resolve of the Privy Council to make a serious effort to accommodate the Greenland fishery dispute. A formal statement of the English grievances was set forth in a letter to the ambassadors, and they were requested, now that far more than the three months' delay which the King had conceded was past, to pay up the indemnity of £22,000 for the losses that had been suffered. The Netherlanders at once replied that they were ready to consider the Greenland differences as soon as the East Indian were settled, but not before. Unless the East Indian negotiations were pushed on, they threatened to return home (October 3). For some two months accordingly the Indies held the field. When, however, the middle of December had arrived the Council once more repeated their demand that the indemnity, which had been promised in 1619, should now be handed over. The envoys denied having any knowledge of such a promise. They would make inquiries about it, meanwhile their instructions only allowed them to discuss the Greenland question as a whole and without prejudice. They asked for proofs of the alleged promise. None were forthcoming. So by raising this side-issue the Dutch achieved their object of gaining time. An accord at last having been reached on East Indian affairs, the envoys announced that after fourteen months' sojourn in London they were unable to remain longer. Caron, they said, would have full powers to carry on negotiations about the Greenland matter. So far as any real settlement of disputes was concerned, the embassy was again a complete failure. Even the accord in the East was a sham. The English Company had obtained a nominal position of equality with its Dutch rival in the Indies, and a definite share of the coveted trade in the Spice islands. But all the power was in the hands of the Dutch, and such an artificial arrangement was more likely, as events were speedily to show, to breed fresh discords than to allay the old ones.

IV: 1623-1629

The embassy of 1622 returned to the Netherlands early in February, 1623. A few weeks later Prince Charles, accompanied by the Duke of Buckingham, was on his way to Madrid to woo in person his prospective Spanish bride. No more conclusive proof could have been shown of the lack of success of Aerssen in obtaining any assurance of armed support from King James for the States in their renewed war with Spain or for the recovery of the Palatinate.

Yet, strangely enough, at this very time of increasing political alienation, four English and two Scottish regiments formed (as indeed was the case throughout the remainder of the eighty years' war) the very kernel of the States army, and campaign after campaign bore the brunt of the fighting. When the Spaniards laid siege to Bergen-op-Zoom in July, 1622, Maurice had reinforced the garrison by fourteen English and Scottish companies. The gallant defence of the town first by Colonel Henderson, then, after this officer fell mortally wounded, by Sir Charles Morgan, excited general admiration in Europe. In October, Spinola, after making repeated and desperate efforts to capture the place, was compelled to raise the siege. These troops were recruited by royal permission in England and Scotland, remained British subjects, and were distinguished by their national uniforms and colours, by the beat of the drum and the march. They were, however, in Dutch pay, and took an oath of allegiance to the States-General, from whom the officers received their commissions.[34]

This same period saw also the beginnings of rivalry in the West as well as in the East. In 1621 a Charter was granted to the Dutch West India Company. This Charter was framed on the model of that of the East India Company, and it was hoped that the new venture might be attended by the same good fortune and phenomenal success as had followed Dutch enterprise in Java and the Malayan Archipelago. Far from being a mere commercial undertaking, it was intended from the first that the West India Company should be required to equip considerable armed forces, naval and military, wherewith to strike a blow at the Spanish power in America, and cut off those sources of revenue which supplied King Philip with the sinews of war. In carrying out such projects of aggression in the Spanish main there was less risk of disputes arising between the Dutch and English than had been the case in the East Indies. Nevertheless, the colonists and traders of the two nationalities were in America also rivals and competitors in the same localities. Netherlanders and Englishmen had already for some years before 1621 been carrying on traffic with the natives and setting up trading posts side by side in the estuary of the Amazon, and in the various river mouths along the coast of Guiana. In 1609, by letters patent, a grant was made by James I to Robert Harcourt, of Stanton Harcourt, in the county of Oxford, for the planting and inhabiting of the whole coast of Guiana between the rivers Amazon and Essequibo, and this grant was renewed to Roger North in 1619, and again by Charles I to the Duke of Buckingham in 1626. Yet within the limits of these grants the Dutch in 1616 established themselves permanently on the river Essequibo, and in 1627 on the river Berbice, while a number of abortive attempts were made to set up trading posts and colonies at other points of this coast. More important than any of these, a settlement had been made in 1614 on the island of Manhattan at the mouth of the Hudson river, a grant having been given at that date by the States-General to a body of Amsterdam merchants of all unoccupied land between Chesapeake Bay and Newfoundland. This settlement and those in Guiana were in 1622 taken over by the newly erected West India Company. Thus in North America the Dutch took possession of the best harbour on the coast, and their colony of New Netherland with its capital New Amsterdam (afterwards New York) was thrust in like a wedge between the English colonies of Virginia and New England. In the West Indian islands and on the Gold Coast of West Africa the keen traders of the two nations also found themselves side by side, with the result in almost all cases, as has been well said, that the Dutch extracted the marrow, leaving the English the bone.[39] It will at once be seen therefore that the activities of the Dutch West India Company, though it came into being primarily for the purpose of 'bearding the King of Spain in his treasure house', were certain, sooner or later, to come into conflict with English enterprise and to enlarge the area within which their respective interests and claims were divergent.

But to return to my immediate subject. The ill-success of the embassy of 1622 in effecting any settlement except the accord relating to the East Indies, an accord which was not regarded in Holland with much favour and which was speedily to prove a failure, caused considerable disquietude to the States. It was resolved therefore to make another real effort to accommodate the old grievances of the English in regard to the acts of violence charged against the Dutch fishermen both on the coast of Scotland and off Spitzbergen. It was hoped that by so doing, any further raising of the question of fishing rights might be avoided. The news of the journey of Prince Charles to Madrid changed disquietude into genuine alarm, lest James, irritated as he was by a succession of fruitless negotiations and long-protracted disputes, might be tempted to cement the Spanish marriage by an alliance with the hereditary foe, and to seek redress against the United Provinces by force of arms. Steps were accordingly taken to enforce strictly the placards by which the skippers of the herring-busses were forbidden under heavy pains and penalties to interfere with or to disturb the Scottish fisherfolk in their industry (April 20, 27, May 6, 1623), and they were also warned not to approach too near to the coast. Caron was requested to inform the English Council of these measures of precaution. The States-General were likewise anxious in their desire to arrive at a friendly understanding that the claims for damages against the Greenland (Northern) Company should be paid. But the old difficulties supervened. The directors of the Greenland Company reminded them of the counterclaim for damages suffered at the hands of the English. To pay therefore the English claim before demanding from the Muscovy Company a simultaneous settlement of Dutch grievances would be, they pointed out, playing into King James's hands. It would be regarded as an admission of his exclusive and particular rights in the Spitzbergen fishery, rights which the Greenland Company and the States had repeatedly refused to acknowledge. So, despite pressure both from Carleton and Caron, the matter dragged on. At last, December 14, a letter was sent to Caron, denying that any promise had been given by the embassy of 1618-9 of a one-sided payment of damages, as stated by the English, but expressing the willingness of the Dutch to make a mutual settlement. As, however, so often before in these negotiations, delay had served its purpose.

When this letter reached Caron, a dramatic change in the English policy had taken place to the advantage of the Netherlands. The negotiations with Spain for the restitution of the Palatinate had broken down. Philip IV and Olivares had never intended to purchase the friendship of England at such a price, and the marriage prospect, on which for so many years his heart had been set, had to be reluctantly abandoned by King James. 'I like not', he said, 'to marry my son with a portion of my daughter's tears.'

The return of the Prince of Wales and the Duke of Buckingham, October 5, angry at the treatment accorded to them at Madrid, led to the overthrow of the party at Court which had favoured a Spanish alliance. Parliament was summoned, and Buckingham in advocating an anti-Spanish policy found himself for once a popular favourite. Pressed by his son, by Buckingham, by Parliament, and by public opinion, the aged King with a heavy heart saw himself compelled to abandon his cherished scheme of recovering the Palatinate by peaceful negotiations, and to take steps for armed intervention. The States-General, on seeing the turn that events were taking, wisely determined to send another embassy to London to take advantage of the opportunity for concluding the wished-for offensive and defensive alliance between England and the United Provinces. There was this time no delay in drawing up the instructions, and Aerssen and Joachimi, the two best men they could have chosen, departed on their mission February 24.

There can be little question that the moving cause for the sending of this embassy with such unusual dispatch is to be found in an interview between Sir Dudley Carleton and Prince Maurice, which the former records in a letter to the Duke of Buckingham dated December 9, 1623.

'I have thought fit', wrote the ambassador, 'to set down at large (whilst it is fresh in my memory) an opportunity as properly given unto me this day by the Prince of Orange (who is the only person of power and confidence we have here to treat withal) as I hope your Grace will think it seasonably taken.'

Some business at the Council of State, at which both were present, having been got through more quickly than was expected, Maurice, so Carleton informed his correspondent,

'gave me a long hour's leisure afterwards in his garden, which he himself desired of me... he asked me bluntly (after his manner) *Qui at'il de vostre mariage?* ⁽ᵃ⁾ I told him it was now at a stay upon this point, that the restitution of the Palatinate must be first concluded. And that the Queen of Bohemia was not only well comforted with this assurance, but pleased herself with a further conceit that the opportunity was never fairer for this State to regain the King her father's favour, and return to the ancient support of his Crowns, which by way of gratitude for her good usage, since she had her refuge into these parts, she could not but admonish his Excellency of and advise him not to let it slip. Here I took occasion to play my own part, and to remember unto him how things had passed within the compass of my experience from the beginning, letting him know what friendship his Majesty had shewed this State in making their truce; what sincerity in rendering their cautionary towns according to contract when they were demanded; what affection in supporting their affairs during their late domestic disputes; what care in settling our East-Indian differences; finally, what patience in conniving at all the misdemeanours and insolences of their seamen without seeking revenge.'

Carleton then proceeds to defend the King's attitude to the Dutch, 'whose ill course, pursued through some years' continuance, bred a deserved distaste in his Majesty'; and his listening on the part of Spain to 'fair overtures of friendship, being continually made and confirmed by the tender of a match.... But (he is careful to add) now the cause is removed, the effect may possibly cease in like manner.' The reply of Maurice was 'that nothing could be more certain than the affection of this State to a Prince embracing their cause of opposition to Spain. And if his Majesty could take that resolution, he might dispose of these their lives and fortunes.' A further discussion led finally to the Prince's declaration, 'When the King would be to this State as Queen Elizabeth was, this State would be to him as it was to Queen Elizabeth.' The advice of Carleton to the Duke is to seize the chance of effecting a good understanding with the Netherlands. 'The present opportunity [to quote the actual words] of the Prince of Orange's good affection, and strength of these provinces both by sea and land as it yet stands, but not possible so long to continue, being seasonably laid hold of, his Majesty may have with this State a firm and fruitful alliance.'

The embassy then, which reached England on February 26, 1624, had a comparatively easy task before it. It was received by the populace with acclamations, and by the King, now completely under the influence of Buckingham, with friendliness and distinction. Even the news of the (so-called) massacre of Amboina in the far East, which was to arouse in England for many years a bitter feeling of resentment against the Dutch, did not now lead to any delay in the negotiations, which proceeded smoothly from the first. Aerssen and Joachimi had English public opinion with them, and a treaty for a defensive alliance between the two countries was signed on June 15. By this treaty James allowed an additional force of 6,000 men to be raised in England, the pay to be at his charges, the States undertaking to refund the amount advanced on the conclusion of a peace or truce. So quickly was the enlistment carried out, that four regiments of 1,500 men each, commanded by the Earls of Oxford, Essex, and Southampton and Lord Willoughby de Eresby, landed in Holland ready for service on July 23. The contingent arrived at an opportune moment, as Spinola had just invaded Dutch Brabant at the head of an army of 24,000 foot and 3,000 horse, and had laid siege to Breda.

This treaty of alliance of June 15, 1624, was followed as a matter of course, by negotiations for a settlement of the long-standing disputes about the Greenland fisheries indemnity and other questions, but despite the efforts of the States-General and the two residents Carleton and Caron, but little progress was made. The directors of the Greenland (Northern) Company had the powerful influence of Amsterdam behind them, and they raised, with the same obstinacy as on previous occasions, strong opposition to making any payment for damages, unless the English agreed to satisfy their counter-claim for losses sustained in 1613 and 1617. Matters were still further delayed by the illness and death of Noel Caron, December 11, 1624. Caron was a real loss at this moment, for he had during fourteen difficult and anxious years filled the post of ambassador of the United Provinces in London with conspicuous industry, ability, and tact. The selection of Albert Joachimi, Lord of Ostend, as his successor was probably the best that could have been made, and met with general approval. He was a man of proved experience, and had been recently in England with Aerssen with the mission that so successfully concluded the treaty. It was intended that he should at once enter upon his duties and take with him to England instructions for a prompt settlement of the Greenland indemnity, if possible by a friendly agreement; if not, in any case 'decisively and authoritatively', and in their turn the other pending disputes and complaints.

Events, however, occurred which effected so complete a change in the political situation that his departure was perforce delayed. On March 27, 1625, James I died. A month later, Maurice, Prince of Orange, breathed his last, April 25, 1625. Charles I ascended the throne of England, and it was hoped this would mean a more decisive intervention of England in foreign politics. The new King was embittered against Spain, and it was known that the Duke of Buckingham, who at this time professed friendship for Holland, and through private pique was even more hostile to the Spaniards than his master, held an influence over him greater even than that which he had exercised over his father. It was largely through his efforts that, after the rupture of the Spanish match, a marriage had been arranged between the Prince of Wales and the sister of Louis XIII. The accomplishment of this union was one of the very first acts of the new reign. Charles and Henrietta Maria were married at Paris by proxy, May 11, and at Canterbury, June 12, with Anglican rites.

Richelieu was now firmly established in power, and in his hands Henry IV's policy of hostility to the ascendancy in Europe of the house of Habsburg was revived. Charles was therefore not without hopes of obtaining armed assistance from France in that war with Spain for the recovery of the Palatinate on which his heart was set. In the United Provinces, Frederick Henry, Prince of Orange, succeeded to all the posts and to more than the influence of his brother. He was, as a general, the equal of Maurice, and was far superior to him as a statesman. During his Stadholderate, strong in the support and affection of all parties and classes, Frederick Henry was able for many years, despite the cumbersome and intricate machinery of government in the

1

Dutch Republic, to exercise a control over the conduct of foreign affairs that was practically undisputed. He, as the son of Louise de Coligny, had throughout his life strong French leanings, and the aim of his diplomacy was from the first to secure the goodwill of Richelieu and the help of French troops and subsidies for the Netherlands. To send Joachimi at such a juncture to London to discuss the settlement of a fishery indemnity was clearly inadequate. It was resolved accordingly that with the newly appointed resident ambassador a special embassy should go to England to congratulate the King upon his accession and his marriage, and, in view of the strained relations between Charles and Spain, to negotiate a treaty between the two countries on the basis of an offensive and defensive alliance. Francis van Aerssen and Rienck van Burmania were chosen as envoys extraordinary for this mission. They set sail, accompanied by Joachimi, on June 16. All the circumstances were favourable to the success of their mission, no difficulties supervened, and on September 17 the treaty of Southampton was signed. By this time a great expedition was being prepared in England for the destruction of the port of Cadiz and the capture of the Plate fleet. Already, efforts had been made by Buckingham to persuade the States to allow 2,000 seasoned English troops in their pay to serve on the great fleet he was equipping, in exchange for 2,000 recruits. But although the 2,000 recruits were sent over (June 19) to Rotterdam, the States-General would not part with their veterans, whose services they sorely needed. Sickness carried off numbers of the raw levies, who were not allowed to land, and the remains had to return in miserable plight to Plymouth at the end of August. Being without pay, these unhappy men had lived during the interval at the personal charges of Sir Dudley Carleton. In a letter to Sir F. Nethersole, secretary to the Queen of Bohemia, dated August 30, the ambassador wrote:

'I have had no small trouble with 2,000 soldiers sent hither out of the North of England to be exchanged with the States for so many old musquettiers, which the weakness of the States' army, especially in the English nation, could not admit, and, having understood his Majesty's intention to use these 2,000 in the service of the fleet, I caused them three weeks since to be embarqued at Rotterdam, where they have layn ever since, attending the wind, but I hope they will now get away.'

Charles, having already quarrelled with his first Parliament, which was dissolved August 12, had failed to obtain the subsidies he required for carrying out his ambitious foreign policy. The States, however, consented to allow General Sir Edward Cecil and several other officers of experience in their service to absent themselves for three months and take part in the expedition against Spain, provided that they took none of their soldiers with them. Cecil, although a land soldier without any naval experience, was induced by Buckingham to take command of the great armada, a post for which he was quite unfitted. The fleet, after many delays, at last set sail October 5, badly equipped, with victuals only for six weeks, foredoomed to failure. In accordance with the terms of the treaty, a squadron of twenty Dutch ships under William of Nassau, a natural son of Maurice, took part in the expedition. There is no need to follow its fortunes further here. 'One by one,' says Dr. Gardiner, 'all through the winter months the shattered remains of the once powerful fleet came staggering home, to seek refuge in whatever port the winds and waves would allow.'

Such an ignominious issue to this great enterprise was of evil omen to the new reign. It was wounding to English pride and roused public indignation against Buckingham to a high pitch. In these circumstances it is not to be wondered at that the alliance between Great Britain and the United Provinces did not prevent a fresh crop of differences arising between them. The massacre of Amboina rankled in the mind of Charles, and it had not been forgotten or forgiven by his people. The right of the English ambassador at the Hague to a seat on the Council of State had strictly ceased when the treaty which granted it came to an end with the close of the truce in 1621. But Dudley Carleton had continued without gainsaying, so long as Maurice lived, to enjoy his former privileges. By a resolution of the States, June 5, 1626, however, he was informed that henceforth he was permitted to take part in the deliberations of the Council not as a right, but simply by courtesy. Carleton attempted to obtain a withdrawal of the resolution, but in vain. As the most important affairs were at this time no longer transacted in the Council of State but in the States-General, the loss of influence was not really great, nevertheless the mere passing of such a resolution when the treaty of Southampton was not yet a year old was resented by the English as a slight. Difficulties had also arisen over the restrictions placed and the duties levied upon the Merchant Adventurers, who had the staple of the English cloth trade at Delft. Worse than all, a number of Dutch merchant vessels had been seized and searched on the ground that they were carrying contraband and trading with the Spanish enemy. The Hollanders throughout the War of Independence had always insisted on the right to freedom of commerce even with their foes, and by supplying the Spaniards not only with food but with arms and munitions, had made immense profits, which helped largely to fill the rebel war-chest. It was the attempt of Leicester to stop this commerce, which chiefly caused his unpopularity in the Netherlands. The treaty of Southampton (arts. 20-23) had forbidden all such traffic, but the keen traders of Amsterdam could not be restrained from the secret evasion of a restriction, to which they had so long refused to submit. Hence acts of reprisal on the part of the English Government, and bitter complaints on both sides.

Once again it was necessary to send a special envoy to London. The chosen ambassador this time was Jacob Cats, better known as the People's Poet of the Netherlands than as a statesman, though he was far from being undistinguished in the latter capacity, seeing that he was to fill for a number of years the important post of Grand Pensionary of Holland. He departed upon his mission March 9, 1627. His object was to negotiate a Navigation Treaty (*traité de Marine*) dealing with the various thorny questions regarding contraband of war and right of search at sea which had been causing so much trouble. But no sooner had the conferences with the Privy Council begun than the Dutch envoy was confronted with complaints that the old outstanding disputes, the indemnities claimed in reparation for the Amboina massacre, and for the acts of violence committed by the herring fishers off the coast of Scotland, and by the whale fishers at Spitzbergen, had never been settled. Cats had to plead that these matters were not included in his instructions, and after some controversy he succeeded in securing the postponement of these obtrusive and troublesome matters. They were at the first suitable opportunity to be discussed with the resident ambassador, Joachimi, who would be furnished with special instructions from the States. The policy of delay, which had proved so successful in the past, once more gained for the Netherlanders all that they required. The fisheries went on, under protest indeed, but undisturbed. The indemnities continued to be claimed, but remained unpaid. The main purpose of Cats's mission was, however, not achieved. No agreement about contraband and right of search and seizure was reached. The comment of Aitzema upon the negotiations is worth reproducing; it is scarcely possible to describe what took place more pithily or with greater acuteness:

'With these and such-like proposals, with plaints and counterplaints, was the time spent, without either the one or the other being made any the wiser. Each one thinks that he is most in the right; everybody looks outwards, nobody homewards, and for much of the time each was taxing the other with offences in which they themselves were the more guilty. The big fishes eat the small ones. He who has the might uses it; every one speaks merely of uprightness, of sincerity, of affection, and there is nothing but deception and hypocrisy on all sides. The English thought also (as was quite true) that they had done much for the common cause and for the Reformed Religion: and that it behoved this State likewise to suffer some inconvenience in their commerce; because otherwise all business which was in England, would find its way to the United Provinces, if these with too great and undisturbed freedom should use the sea, and not the English. Thus the Ministers of this State did not accomplish much. To Heer Cats, however, an honourable farewell was accorded with the usual present, and the dignity of Knighthood. He returned to the Hague August 30.'

The spring of 1627 had found the Government of Charles I involved in so many difficulties that it is not surprising that the King should not have found it possible to take any decisive line in his negotiations with the Dutch. He had quarrelled with his Parliament, and knew not where to turn to raise the money to meet the heavy liabilities in which he had involved himself. The attack on Cadiz had utterly miscarried, and had failed to give any help to the cause of the Palatinate. At this moment of sore disappointment he had seen with misgiving that the new Stadholder, Frederick Henry, and his minister Aerssen, had turned to France with friendly overtures, and had found Richelieu willing to receive them. France had promised to the States a yearly subsidy, and a loan of troops on condition that the Dutch would send a squadron to assist in the blockade of La Rochelle, and would undertake not to conclude a peace or truce with Spain without the knowledge and consent of the French King. Charles felt that his strenuous efforts to increase his fleet and render it more efficient, with the aim of making the English navy supreme in the Channel and the North Sea, were directly threatened by such an alliance. It was known that it was the policy of Richelieu to strengthen the position of France as a maritime power, and the traditional English jealousy of French aggrandizement was increased rather than diminished by the close bond which united the royal families. The French marriage had always been unpopular in England, great resentment being felt at the concessions that had been made with regard to the public performance of Roman Catholic rites. Charles himself found the position of things at Court so difficult that he was obliged finally to take the strong step of sending back the French attendants of the young Queen. This gave great offence at Paris, and the soreness between the two countries was aggravated by the high-handed action of the English on the sea during the Spanish war. French ships had been searched and seized, and in reprisals an embargo had been laid upon English vessels and goods at La Rochelle and other places. Finally, the countries drifted into war. Charles hoped that he might secure the friendly neutrality of Spain, but his efforts failed, and Spain allied herself with France.

In June a great expedition sailed under the command of Buckingham to relieve La Rochelle. To meet its cost without the help of his Parliament, Charles had been compelled to have recourse to forced loans and other unpopular expedients, and the issue was to be a disaster even more humiliating than that of Cadiz. In these circumstances, while this fleet in the spring of 1627 was being prepared, but its destiny still unknown, it was necessary for the King to keep on good terms with the United Provinces, and to pursue a temporizing policy with regard to the grievances that he had against them. While therefore Jacob Cats, as special ambassador from the States, was busily engaged in negotiations with the English Government in London, Charles sent on his part an envoy extraordinary to the Hague, nominally for the presentation of the Order of the Garter to the Prince of Orange, in reality to sound the disposition of the Dutch Statesmen and to make proposals to them.

The man selected to carry out this commission was the former ambassador at the Hague, Sir Dudley (now Lord) Carleton, who had returned to London in the previous year. In his secret instructions (dated May, 1627) are several interesting passages.[37] The document opens thus:—

'The mayne scope of your imployment consisting of two points; the one to prevent the practices of the French, who seeke by presentation of new treatyes, and profers of summes of money, to make, as it were, a purchase of the affection of that State, and to gaine it from us; the other, to provide that no misunderstanding growe upon such overtures of pacification as are made unto us by the Spanyard; we may well consider that in cases of this nature, with people so composed as they are, there is required a very cautious proceeding.... We would have you begin with declaration of our purpose constantly to continue our preparations against Spayne, as against a common enemie, in conformity to the league, offensive and defensive, betwixt us and that State, and to make the same more manifest, you shall have a list of the Shipping now sett out under our High Admiral, the Duke of Buckingham, with such as we are now further preparing for the security of these seas; and hereupon you are to require them to arme, in like manner extraordinarely to sea, according to treaty....'

Thus was Carleton to attempt to blind the Dutch statesmen as to the overtures that had been made to Spain and as to the purpose of the fleet gathered at Portsmouth. With regard to the second point, the instructions proceed:—

'We would have you take knowledge of such griefs and discontentments, as their resident Ambassador Joachimi, and Catz their extraordinary deputy, have complained of against our seamen, and thereupon make knowen the charge (wherewith you are well acquainted) we have given certaine select persons of our Council to treat with them, of all due and reasonable satisfaction for what is past, and a reglement for the future; but with all you are to remember unto them, that, as we are to have a care of their contentments, so we are not to neglect the protection we owe to our own subjects.'

And then follows a setting out of the old grievances, the Amboina affair and the differences between the East India Companies generally, and the exactions upon the Merchant Adventurers now having their Court in the staple town of Delft under the title of tare. There is no mention here of the fisheries. As regards the choice of friendship with France or with England, the instruction, after a recitation of all that the Republic has owed to English goodwill in the past, thus presents the alternative:—

'Therefore, as things may growe to greate extremity betwixt us and the French King, in case you find no disposition in the States to joyne with us in assistance, as their enemys do with France, we like well you should persuade them to hold themselves neutrall, whereby to reserve to themselves the liberty of mediation of attonement, to which we shall be at all times ready to lend a willing ear to them, as common friends. And as they may apprehend danger to their State, by want of such pecuniary ayde as is verbally presented to them by the French King as the price of their affections; or may be prest to the renewing of the triennial treaty of Compiegne, let them in their wisdomes, waigh what is the less of evils, in forbearing for a while the acceptation of the weak and faltering friendship of France, which, being in warre with England, cannot have meanes to assist them, though never so willing and constant; or provoking England to the necessity of conjoyning with their enemies, for which they cannot but know the doore is allways open to us; and then consider that when the flame betwixt France and us hath no such fewell from this country as is ministered to the French from Spayne, it will be the sooner extinguished and these crownes may be quickly reunited, not only to their ayde as formerly, but likewise to the support and restitution of such friends in Germany, in whose welfare they, with us, have common interest....'

Finally, Carleton is requested to remonstrate with the States for the difficulties they had raised to the admission of his successor at the Hague—a nephew, named Dudley Carleton like himself—to a seat in the Council of State, which had always hitherto been granted to all English ambassadors and agents since 1585.

Carleton had his first audience in the assembly of the States-General, June 14/24, and a second five days later. In the first he read an address setting forth the various objects of his diplomatic mission; in the second he asked permission of the States for the Prince of Orange to accept the Garter. In a letter dated June 27 (o.s.), to Lord Killultagh, the ambassador gives an account of a conference that he had with a deputation of the States-General, consisting of one member representing each province. 'He laid open to them', he writes, 'all that had passed from the beginning to the end', and tried to persuade them of the advantage of clinging to the English in preference to the French alliance. He found it, however, a difficult task to remove the apprehensions that were felt that Charles's quarrel with France meant a drawing nearer to Spain. Carleton, at the same time, does not scruple to point out that the fact that he has gone to Holland without any money to pay even interest on the expenses that had been incurred by the States for the maintenance of Mansfeld's English levies in 1625, or for the creditors of the Queen of Bohemia, or for preventing the forfeiture of 'His Majesty's Jewells, which are in pawn at Amsterdam', would be ruinous to his mission, and begs for the necessary cash to be sent. The money, it is needless to say, was not forthcoming, and such was the suspicion against England that, despite Carleton's efforts to secure for the English resident ambassador a seat on the Council of State, the proposal was rejected by the vote of every province separately. Nevertheless there was genuine alarm in the Netherlands that the continuance of the war between France and England would be injurious to their interests by forcing one of the combatants to seek the alliance of Spain. The missions of Cats to England and of Carleton to the Hague, though they failed in bringing about any real settlement of the differences between the two powers, at least effected an understanding that, for a time at any rate, grievances were not to be pressed. The interests of Dutch trade rendered the undisturbed passage of the Channel, free from interference by hostile fleets or cruisers, a consideration of the very utmost importance.

It was resolved, therefore, to send yet another special embassy to England to offer the mediation of the States between the belligerent powers, and to negotiate for the release of the many Dutch ships which had been seized on the high seas and kept in English harbours. The lord of Randwijk and Adrian Pauw, pensionary of Amsterdam, were accordingly sent. They arrived in London, January 25, 1628, and stayed in England some fourteen months. Carleton meantime remained at the Hague. In May of this same year the Earl of Carlisle joined him, bringing further instructions from the King. By these instructions he was bidden to assist Carleton in pressing upon the States the advantages of friendship with England in preference to France, and the necessity, if they wished to obtain it, of forbidding the construction of French war-vessels in the Dutch ports, and of punishing adequately the perpetrators of 'the foule and bloody fact' of Amboina. It will thus be seen that diplomacy during these years 1627 and 1628 was indeed busy, so busy that it is by no means easy to see light clearly amidst such a tangled web of negotiations. This is certain, that they had small result. The Prince of Orange, and his chief adviser Francis van Aerssen, had made the French alliance the sheet-anchor of their policy. They wished to be on friendly terms with England, and to bring the war, which was so injurious to Dutch interests, to a speedy conclusion, but they distrusted the intentions of Charles I, and knew that the breach with his Parliament in any case must deprive him of the resources for carrying out any bold and active intervention in the German war. They suspected, moreover, that it was not unlikely that Charles might follow in his father's footsteps and strive to help his relatives in the Palatinate by means of negotiations with Spain rather than by hostilities against that power. The efforts of Carleton and Carlisle met therefore with little or no success. The influence of Amsterdam in the States of Holland was too strong for any steps to be taken to punish those who had been concerned in the Amboina tragedy, and the English demands were met by evasion and delay. But though Carleton was unsuccessful, the envoys in London, in carrying out their task as mediators between England and France, were helped by the pressure upon Charles of the financial difficulties in which, after the assassination of Buckingham (August 23, 1628), he was becoming more and more involved. The dissolution of March, 1629, was a final breach with his Parliament. The King had therefore little or no alternative but to bring his war with France to a speedy conclusion. The Dutch envoys, on their part, did their best to remove the obstacles to an Anglo-French understanding, and peace was signed April 24, 1629.

———————————————————

V: 1629-1641

The foreign policy of Charles I during the eleven years of autocratic rule which followed the dissolution of Parliament in 1629, was conditioned by his lack of money. His schemes were ambitious and were obstinately pursued, and the charge that has frequently been preferred against him of inconstancy and fickleness, though it has a basis of truth, is on the whole unjust. Charles's projects had to be frequently modified, because he found himself without the means for carrying them out. In November, 1630, peace was concluded with Spain. It was his dearest desire to see the Palatinate restored to the Elector Frederick, and his sister, to whom he was much attached, freed from the necessity of living as an exile in Holland; but the cost of a military expedition to the aid of the Protestants in Germany was prohibitive. He was also suspicious of French motives and of the policy underlying their alliance with the Dutch. Perhaps at this time the predominant idea before Charles's mind was the restoration of the navy to a position of supremacy in the British seas. His most earnest endeavours were for some years directed to this end, but its attainment was seriously threatened by the close bonds which united the powerful fleets of the Dutch Republic with the growing naval strength of France.

In these circumstances, he attempted to pursue his father's policy of seeking to counterbalance the Franco-Dutch alliance by a good understanding with Spain, through whose intervention with the Emperor he hoped he might be able to secure for Frederick V some portion at any rate of his ancestral possessions. In 1631 a treaty with Spain for the partition of the Netherlands was actually drawn up, but it came to nothing, and its failure was followed by negotiations with Gustavus Adolphus. These also were fruitless, for Charles was unable to offer the Swedish King the military assistance without which the proffered alliance had no value. Hopes, however, no doubt lingered in Charles's mind that the phenomenal success of Gustavus would lead to the restoration of the Elector Palatine to his rights, but Gustavus was slain at Lützen (November, 1632), and the disastrous defeat of the Swedes and their Protestant allies at Nördlingen (August, 1634) gave a decisive superiority in Germany to the Hispano-Imperialist forces. The Habsburg family alliance had for the time completely gained the upper hand.

Charles, who had been tentatively making overtures to France, now turned once more to Spain (October, 1634) with a fresh scheme for the partition of the Netherlands, and though the time was now past for any real change in Spanish policy, a treaty was actually signed (May 1, 1635) by which the English King agreed to assist the Spaniards with a naval force against the Dutch. He had been impelled to take this step from fear of French designs. The battle of Nördlingen had had the effect of drawing the French and Dutch nearer together in the common dread of a Habsburg predominance. A treaty of subsidies was at once agreed upon, and it was followed

(February, 1635) by an offensive and defensive alliance between the two powers. Both France and the United Provinces bound themselves not to make a separate peace, and it was provided that the Spanish Netherlands—the southern provinces, by the death of the Archduchess Isabel, had in 1633 reverted to Spain—should be conquered and partitioned between the two contracting parties. Charles had therefore looked to a Spanish alliance as a counterpoise to a Franco-Dutch supremacy in the 'narrow seas'. He hoped also that he might at the same time secure favourable terms for his nephew—Frederick V had died in November, 1632—in the Palatinate. He was soon to learn by the publication of the Treaty of Prague (May 30, 1635) that the Emperor had transferred the territory and the electoral dignity of the Palatinate to the Duke of Bavaria. Direct negotiations with Vienna, backed, as they were, by no force, were barren, and Charles was compelled to see in the aid of France, who had concluded an offensive and defensive alliance with the Swedes, two months after that with the States, his only hope for the furtherance of his nephew's interests. Richelieu had now definitely ranged himself with the two leading Protestant powers in a league against the house of Austria, and had pledged all the military and financial resources of France to the task of carrying out the policy of Henry IV, which a quarter of a century before had been rendered abortive by the dagger of Ravaillac.

The States judged this to be a fitting time to send over to England a special envoy, and Cornelis van Beveren, lord of Strevelshoek, was selected for the post. He set out for London, March 19, 1636. His instructions were to act in concert with Joachimi and the French ambassador De Senneterre, in urging Charles to join in a triple bond with the United Provinces and France for the purpose of making a combined attack upon Spain. Van Beveren was to point out that only by such a course could he lend any effectual assistance to his nephew. It was hoped that Charles Lewis, who was now residing at the English Court, would use all his influence in forwarding the objects of the mission.

The negotiations, however, were doomed to take a very different direction from what had been intended. On April 5 the Secretaries of State, Windebank and Coke, came to Van Beveren with a communication from the King. It was to the effect that Charles was preparing to send out a fleet 'to preserve and maintain his sovereignty and hereditary rights over the sea, and for the preservation and protection of commerce', and the Dutch envoy was informed that no one would in future be allowed 'to fish in the King's seas without express licence and suitable acknowledgement.' So long a time had elapsed since the last attempt at interference with the Dutch fishing that all mention of it had been omitted from the instructions of Van Beveren; it was hoped, indeed, that the question would not be revived. On Van Beveren expressing his astonishment at this sudden change of policy, and asking for the reasons which had prompted it, he was referred to the recently published *Mare Clausum seu Dominium Maris*, by John Selden, in which he would find a complete exposition of the King's rights and of the object he had in asserting them. This famous work, written originally, as the author himself tells us, at the command of James I, to establish the claims of the King to the exclusive sovereignty of the British seas, had for some years remained unprinted. The attention of Charles having been drawn to it, he read it carefully, and immediately commanded its publication. Its appearance in December, 1635, had thus an official character, for its principles and policy were henceforth adopted by Charles, as matters demonstrated by irrefutable proofs, and they were endorsed by English public opinion wherever Selden's treatise, which rapidly passed through two editions, was read.

Van Beveren, seriously disturbed, at once wrote home for further instructions, and his fears were not allayed when at an audience, April 15, the King declined the proffered alliance, and expressed his wish for a discussion of the question of maritime rights. His dispatch at this very time of Thomas Howard, Earl of Arundel, on a special mission to Vienna, showed indeed that he still trusted to the result of direct negotiations with the Emperor. Arundel had to pass through Holland, where his presence on such an errand warned the Dutch that the attitude of Charles was anything but friendly, and that grave dangers might be threatening them. In these circumstances the States-General, leaving Van Beveren to continue his negotiations in England, summoned Joachimi to the Hague to consult with them as to the course it was best to take should Charles persist in his purpose. They had need of his advice, for May 10/20, 1636, a proclamation was issued by the King—'for restraint of Fishing upon His Majesty's Seas and Coasts without licence'—which plainly stated the King's intention 'to keepe such a competent strength of shipping upon Our Seas, as may by God's Blessing be sufficient, both to hinder further encroachments on Our Regalities, and assist and protect those our good Friends and Allies, who shall, henceforth, by vertue of Our Licences (to be first obtained) endeavour to take the benefit of Fishing upon our Coasts and Seas, in the places accustomed.'[38]

For some weeks no steps were taken to enforce the proclamation, but on July 20 news reached Van Beveren that an English fleet of fifteen vessels was ready to sail to the fishing-grounds with orders to seize as prizes any boats that refused to pay the toll. To plead for delay was the only course open to the Dutch envoy. He had an interview with the King in person at Windsor, July 27, but was able to effect nothing. Charles assured him that the object of the fleet, so far from being hostile, was intended for the protection of the fisher-folk especially against the Dunkirk pirates (from whose daring attacks they had as a matter of fact suffered much during the past few years), and that the payment of a small toll was but a recognition of the benefit they would receive. With this doubtful assurance he had perforce to rest content. On July 31 twelve ships under Vice-Admiral Pennington actually sailed northwards, and compelled the fishermen that they encountered—most of the boats had already returned home, it being late in the season—to pay the toll. No opposition was made. One of the captains of the Dutch guard-ships had, however, in consequence of his protest against these proceedings, been taken prisoner.

The Dutch Government on hearing this news took decided action. Joachimi was ordered at once to return to England, and as soon as possible to seek an audience with the King. Armed with instructions, Joachimi accordingly left Holland, August 18, convoyed by a fleet under Lieutenant-Admiral Van Dorp. He landed at Southwold, and finding that Charles was at Woodstock he made his way at once to that place. The interview took place September 3.

In accordance with his instructions the ambassador expressed their High Mightinesses astonishment that an Armada should have appeared in the midst 'of the poor fishers and herring-catchers of these lands', and had seized one of the captains of the guard-ships and caused such terror among the fisher-folk that the larger part of them had fled and dared no longer pursue their avocation. His Majesty was courteously requested to withdraw his demand for a licence and to allow the fishers to ply their trade as heretofore, and it was proposed that a conference should be held to consider the fishery question in its entirety. Joachimi did not neglect the opportunity of pointing out how closely the questions of the fisheries and of the Palatinate hung together. Charles was unmoved by these representations, and finally, September 9, declined the proposal of a conference. 'There could be no debating', he said, 'about his Majesty's rights already confirmed publickly before all the world'. The recognition of his rights was a condition which must precede negotiation. After discussion with Van Beveren, seeing that the situation was serious, Joachimi determined to return to the Hague. His start was, however, delayed by various causes, and he did not make his appearance before the States-General until November 22.

Meanwhile the aspect of affairs had not improved. Admiral Van Dorp, who had in the middle of August convoyed Joachimi to England, also had his instructions. He was first to sail with his fleet to the fishing grounds to prevent any injury being done to the fishermen. This accomplished, he was to blockade Dunkirk, and to destroy any privateers or Spanish ships cruising in the Channel. His orders were strict, that he was not to allow his ships to be visited or searched, and during his blockade of Dunkirk he was to keep a watchful eye upon the fisheries of the land and to protect them against the Spaniards or any others who should wish to molest them. These instructions were in fact a direct reply and challenge to the proclamation of King Charles.

The Dutch herring fleet having recovered from their alarm had ventured out, as was their custom, about the middle of September, to the English coasts for a second catch of fish. The Earl of Northumberland had been charged with the collection of the toll from them. He had, however, at this time but three ships with him, and learning that a Dutch squadron of sixteen sail was near at hand he promptly sent for reinforcements. In response, twelve vessels were dispatched from the Thames, October 8. Actual hostilities, however, did not take place. One large detachment of 'busses', not having a sufficient convoy, was made to pay, the rest were left unmolested. The English commander finding himself in the presence of thirteen Dutch war-ships did not venture to attack them. Both sides showed in fact more caution than aggressiveness. The authorities in Holland, however, did not approve Van Dorp's attitude and conduct, and he was requested to resign his command.

The course of events was fortunately to relieve a strain that was rapidly approaching the breaking point. Charles's negotiations with the Emperor had led to no satisfactory result. It was at last made clear to him that by this means there was no hope of obtaining a restoration of the Palatinate. Van Beveren seized the opportunity of placing himself in communication with Charles Lewis, at this time residing in London, with the hope of securing through his aid a better understanding between England and the States. Charles Lewis was only too willing in his own interests to act as intermediatory, and his influence with his uncle was great. His mother, the Queen of Bohemia, was at this time writing pressing letters to her brother begging for his active intervention, and it was urged upon King Charles that the assistance of the Dutch army and navy would be far more valuable to him than any sum of money that could be extracted in the shape of toll from the fisher fleet. On the point of the toll the King showed himself not unwilling to yield, but not one inch would he concede of his claims to the undisputed sovereignty of the sea. If he withdrew his proclamation and allowed the Dutch, as heretofore, freedom of fishing without licence, it would be in compensation for services rendered in the cause of the Palatinate, not as a right based upon ancient treaties and long usage. The Dutch, on the other hand, were keenly alive to all that was involved in any admission of such a dominion of the sea as that claimed by the English King, and were determined not to grant it. On Charles's side, however, financial difficulties at this time rendered any straightforward course impracticable. The King had not the means to fit out an expedition for the help of his nephew, and he hovered hither and thither between divergent policies in the vain hope that without recourse to a Parliament he could find some way of furthering the cause of Charles Lewis, without involving himself in an outlay that he was unable to meet. Scheme after scheme floated before his mind, all of them equally visionary when confronted with the stern realities of impecuniousness. From Ferdinand and Philip he turned to Richelieu. The French armies were advancing in Lorraine and Elsass, and were co-operating with the Dutch in the Netherlands, and with the Swedes and their Protestant allies in Germany. For awhile it appeared as if Richelieu were inclined to an English alliance. In February and March, 1637, a treaty was indeed actually drawn up. It is strongly suspected, however, that the Cardinal was never in real earnest, and only wished to amuse the English King with negotiations, and thus at any rate keep him back from purchasing Spain's goodwill on the Rhine by an offer to take part in a joint naval attack upon the United Provinces. Charles was quite aware of the solidarity of the bond which united France and the States, and that a French alliance implied friendly relations with the Dutch. On February 13 therefore he sent the Secretary of

State, Coke, to Van Beveren, who was still in London, to reopen direct negotiations. It was now proposed that there should be a combined Anglo-Dutch naval expedition in which a French squadron should be invited to participate, which, after driving the Spanish fleets from the sea, should effect a landing in the Peninsula and dictate terms to Philip IV. Meanwhile the King expressed his willingness to allow the Dutch fishermen to pursue their industry along the coasts of his kingdoms freely and without hindrance. During the following season the English fleet would blockade the Flemish ports, but would not appear on the fishing grounds nor make any demands for licences. But with this latter concession the States were not satisfied. Such an act of toleration implied that Charles maintained to the full his claim to the undisputed sovereignty of the sea. He would not during the time of the allied operations press his rights to issue licences and exact toll, he only waived them as a favour. Further than this he could not go. On the question of the *dominium maris*, despite the earnest entreaties of Charles Lewis, he refused any compromise. But on the other side there was no less obstinacy. The Prince of Orange himself wrote (March 1) to Van Beveren, that he was on no account to commit himself or assent to any terms unless the proclamation concerning the fishing licences was first withdrawn. With France the negotiations for an alliance appeared to be proceeding smoothly, the treaty lay ready for signature, and on March 4 Charles sent full powers to his ambassador at Paris to conclude the matter. On the 23rd came the news that difficulties had arisen, and that France also required that the proclamation should be withdrawn, at least during the period of the treaty. But Charles, though the negotiations still dragged on, absolutely declined to discuss a question which concerned his rights and honour, and so he now once more lent a not unwilling ear to the tempting offers made to him by the Spanish ambassador. Spain was willing in return for an offensive and defensive alliance against the United Provinces to recognize the King's sovereign rights on the seas, and to hand over at once the Lower Palatinate. They even went so far as to promise the surrender of certain towns in Flanders as pledges for the ultimate restitution of the Upper Palatinate and the electoral dignity to Charles Lewis. It is extremely doubtful whether these proposals were serious, in any case they were not seriously entertained.

The mere prospect of an Anglo-Spanish agreement had, however, the effect which Charles probably intended it to have in making the French and Dutch more conciliatory. Negotiations were resumed, and the fishery question by mutual consent was relegated to the background. It was finally arranged that a conference should be held at Hamburg at the end of June to settle the terms of a quadruple alliance between France, England, the United Provinces, and Sweden. Terms of peace were to be laid before the Emperor by the four powers conjointly. In case of their rejection the King of England was to declare war against Austria and Spain. Everything now seemed to be working smoothly, and no one doubted that the conference would meet and that its issue would be favourable. The Dutch fishermen had not been interfered with, and such was the confidence in the States that England had now finally thrown in her lot with the coalition against the house of Austria, that instructions were sent to Van Beveren to return home where his presence was required.

Nevertheless the Dutch after his recall did not show any eagerness to proceed. Reflection made them doubtful about Charles's bona fides. They misliked the high pretensions of the English to the sovereignty of the seas, for in his insistence on this point the King was but voicing the sentiment of his people. It was becoming a really grave issue of practical politics. With astonishment the Dutch learnt that Charles had even given a patent granting exclusive rights of fishing off the shores of Newfoundland, and had forbidden foreigners to fish in those waters without his licence, April, 1637. If he claimed the right to do this, where was the line to be drawn? Under pressure from their French allies, Charles van Cracauw, the ambassador of the States in Denmark, was at length appointed to represent the United Provinces at the Hamburg Conference, but his instructions were not drawn up, and he continued to reside for some time longer in Copenhagen. Throughout the whole of 1637 the Dutch could not be moved to take any further steps in the matter. In the letters of Hugo Grotius (at this time Swedish resident ambassador at Paris) to the Chancellor Axel Oxenstierna many interesting references are made to the attitude of the States, and it must be remembered that Grotius not only had access to the best sources of information, but had an unrivalled acquaintance with the question which was uppermost in the minds of all Dutch statesmen, the freedom of the sea and of the fisheries. On June 4, the very day after the nomination of Cracauw as delegate for the conference, Grotius writes:—

'The ambassador of the States in England informs me that the Spaniards there have great power—that they wish that the restitution of the Palatinate should be regarded as a certain thing; that they promise aid for the safeguarding of the possession of the sea against the Dutch. Would that these things were not true! The same adds that proposals were made by the Spaniards that after the death of this Bavarian the electoral law should be altered, conditions even offered by the Spaniard to the English, if they could be dragged into war against the Dutch Republic, which however I do not fear. For I see that the action of the English is principally directed to the aim of having their commerce into all nations free and to deprive others of theirs. The Dutch had formed a hope that the contest about the fishery would this year be at rest; but I see that the English envoys, who are here [at Paris] hold that for uncertain.'

A fortnight later (June 18) occurs the following passage:—

'After I had written this there came to me the English Envoy Extraordinary, Lord Leicester.... He says, that Northumberland (to whom he is nearly related) is again about to disturb the Dutch in their liberty of using the sea, unless the Dutch purchase it by great services to the Palatine house and by declarations not injurious to English rights. I, restraining myself from a definite declaration about the controversy, have been content to demonstrate, how necessary liberty of fishing was to that Republic and how necessary the Republic itself to the security of all Europe.[19]

Such being the feelings and the relations subsisting between the two countries, it can excite no astonishment that the States were exceedingly cautious before committing themselves to an alliance, which might entail further sacrifice upon them, and tie their hands in a matter of primary importance to their welfare. According to Grotius, proposals were made for holding the conference at the Hague instead of

Hamburg, in order to make sure of Dutch co-operation. But they came to nothing. Charles, however, in the spring of 1638 appears to have been really in earnest. Again and again the English Resident at the Hague appeared before the States-General to urge them to send a representative to the conference. Not, however, until fresh pressure had been put upon them in the name of France and Sweden by the French ambassador, D'Estampes, were definite orders sent to Van Cracauw to go to Hamburg, April 8. Even now he did not have any powers given to him to negotiate as plenipotentiary, but was required to refer all matters to the States-General for their decision. Already, on March 4, a new treaty had been concluded between France and Sweden for the joint prosecution of the war, but the quadruple alliance was never accomplished. Difficulties and intrigues prevented the ratification either of the Anglo-French or Anglo-Swedish Treaties, and the States were more than half-hearted in the business. The ill success of the young Elector Palatine, who had taken the field in the spring of this year at the head of a force raised by the help of his uncle Charles I, virtually brought the conference to an end. Charles Lewis's army was completely defeated at Lemco on October 8. Differences, which had been for some little time endangering the friendly relations of England and France, now came to a head.[40] The representatives of the powers gathered at Hamburg, only to disperse without result. The long drawn out negotiations gave birth to nothing but sterile discussions. The outbreak, indeed, of the troubles in Scotland regarding 'Laud's Liturgy', and the resistance that was being offered to the collection of ship-money, effectually crippled Charles's efforts on behalf of his nephew in Germany. Richelieu no longer saw any advantage in tying his hands by entering into an alliance which promised so little. He preferred therefore to cut himself adrift from the English connexion, and to trust to his alliances with Sweden and the United Provinces[41] for pushing on the war vigorously. It was not for Protestantism that he was fighting, but for the aggrandizement of France at the cost of the House of Habsburg.

This failure of his efforts to bring about, in conjunction with France, a coalition of the Protestant powers for the reconquest of the Palatinate and the restoration of his nephew to his electoral dignity and possessions, made Charles turn his eyes once more to Spain. The presence at the English Court of Mary de Medicis and the Duchess de Chevreuse in 1638 gave fresh life to that party, who had always favoured a Spanish alliance. The news that the Spaniards were making great preparations for a determined attack upon the United Provinces led the King to hope that, despite previous disappointments, he might be able to forward by friendly negotiations with Spain the cause of Charles Lewis. The help of the English fleet could not but be serviceable to a Spanish naval expedition, and possibly Charles had visions of being able to attain through this means that undisputed sovereignty of the British seas which, since the publication of Selden's book, he had set before himself, as we have seen, as one of the chief and unchangeable objects of his policy, and at the same time, perhaps, the pecuniary assistance he so much needed for the suppression of the Scottish rebellion against his authority. With characteristic uncertainty and wavering, however, while negotiating with Spain, the King did not cease his endeavours to gain French support for his nephew. The Spanish preparations caused uneasiness in Paris, as well as at the Hague, and the English fleet was an asset not to be despised in the event of a Spanish armada threatening to dominate the Channel. The death of Duke Bernhard of Saxe-Weimar in July, 1639, left the powerful force of mercenaries which he had commanded without a leader. Charles wished to buy their services for the Elector Palatine, but he could only do this through the good offices of Richelieu, who was already offering good terms to the 'Bernardines' to enter the French service. A treaty between the French Government and the chief officers of the 'Bernardine' army was in fact on the point of being concluded, when Charles Lewis made his appearance at the head-quarters with a supply of English money and tried to induce the leaders to place themselves under his command, as an independent force. The result was his immediate arrest by Richelieu's command, October, 1639. He was imprisoned at Vincennes for several months. This act was a final breach of good relations between France and England.

Meanwhile Charles's approaches to Spain had been equally unfortunate. The Cardinal Infant, Ferdinand, the victor of Nördlingen, had, as Governor-General of the Netherlands, been successful in the conduct of the war against the Dutch and French in the years 1638 and 1639. In the latter year Olivares determined to dispatch a powerful Spanish reinforcement by sea to the Netherlands to take part in the next campaign. Accordingly, early in September, a fleet left the Spanish ports consisting of seventy-seven vessels, many of them of the largest size, commanded by a veteran admiral who had seen much service, Antonio de Oquendo. Its object was to disembark at Dunkirk an expeditionary force of 10,000 men. A Dutch squadron had been cruising in the Channel all the summer, keenly on the look-out for the Spaniards, under the command of Lieutenant-Admiral Martin Harpertzoon Tromp. On September 16 he sighted the armada. He had with him at the moment only thirteen ships. But without hesitation he fiercely attacked the Spaniards, and after a tremendous fight he forced Oquendo to fly for refuge to the English coast. Oquendo, after passing through the Straits of Dover, anchored under the lee of the Downs, side by side with an English squadron of ten ships under Vice-Admiral Pennington. Tromp sent at once urgent messages to Holland for reinforcements. With a squadron that joined him from Dunkirk he lay in the offing blockading the Spanish fleet in the Downs. In all the harbours of Holland and Zeeland the greatest efforts were now made to send every available ship to sea at the earliest moment. Day by day Tromp's fleet increased in number. His orders were uncompromising. He was to attack the Spaniards wherever he found them, as soon as he was in a position to do so with success. Accordingly, on October 21, being now at the head of a fleet of 105 sail with 12 fireships, the Dutch admiral, although the Spaniards still lay in English waters, resolved to take the offensive. Detaching thirty ships under Vice-Admiral De With to watch Pennington, he sailed straight for the enemy's galleons as they sheltered under the cliffs between Dover and Deal. The contest was sharp, but decisive. Under cover of a fog, Oquendo himself with seven vessels made his way to Dunkirk. All the rest were captured or destroyed. Some 15,000 Spaniards perished, about 1,800 were taken prisoners. The Dutch only lost two ships and about 100 killed and wounded. Tromp had won one of the most crushing of naval victories, and had annihilated the power of Spain upon the sea.

This daring infringement of English neutrality could not but give deep offence to King Charles, and be hurtful to the feelings of the English people. It was at once felt in the States that an explanation must be offered for the instructions given to Tromp, which had been so successfully carried out. It was accordingly resolved to dispatch a special envoy to London, and Francis van Aerssen (now generally known as Lord of Sommelsdijk) was himself chosen to undertake the difficult mission. His instructions were that he should complain of the help frequently afforded to the Spaniards by the English, and plead that the attack of Tromp at the Downs was a necessary sequel to the previous encounter from which the Spanish fleet had fled to seek refuge in English waters, and that it was justified by Art. 15 of the Treaty of Southampton. He was further to express the readiness of the States to conclude with the King a fresh treaty of alliance. Sommelsdijk found everything against him. The King was very angry at the gross affront to his honour and his sovereignty of the seas, and the most influential of his counsellors, among them Strafford and Laud, were strongly anti-Dutch. The affair was made an excuse for pressing forward the collection of ship-money, and the Spanish party continually gained strength. The Queen-Mother of France and Madame Chevreuse, who were then at the English Court, did their utmost to further the cause of Spain, and there was talk of cementing an alliance by the marriage of the Princess Royal with the heir to the Spanish crown.

Sommelsdijk, finding he could effect no good result, asked permission to return to Holland.[42] He probably knew that Charles was anxious not to break with the States, for his request brought about a change in the King's demeanour. Charles requested him to remain, and showed himself more friendly. On January 16 the ambassador, whose correspondence with Frederick Henry at this time is of great interest, wrote to the Stadholder that he was not without some hopes now of soothing the resentment of the King by abstaining as far as possible from the irritating topic of the Downs, and letting it fall into oblivion by drawing his attention to other subjects of discussion. Sommelsdijk had persuasive manners, and by the exercise of patience, tact, and conciliation, he did succeed to a large extent in his aim. He was much helped in his task by another negotiation which was now set on foot. Frederick Henry, in this same month of January, 1640, sent over a secret envoy, Jan van der Kerkhoven, Lord of Heenvliet, to propose a marriage between his only son and an English princess. The matter had been first suggested by Marie de Medicis during a visit to the Hague in

1638. The proposal was favourably received, and became the ground for a long-continued struggle between the Spanish and the Franco-Dutch factions at Court. In the meantime, gradually 'the bitterness of the pill' of the Downs was 'sweetened' by marriage negotiations, and the 'scandal' of the infringement of the King's sovereignty over his own waters was, if not forgiven, at least overlooked.

The King saw in fact that it was wiser to keep silence. Spain was clearly a broken reed, and the Dutch had given a signal proof of their possession of a naval strength that it would be dangerous to challenge. Sommelsdijk was quite content on his part to let the matter drop. On February 8, 1646, he wrote to the Stadholder[43]:—

'The scandal of the Downs has been so thoroughly justified, that the greater part of the Council, in the presence of the King, has sustained that we both could and were obliged to do it; so it is sufficiently lulled to sleep, seeing that up to now there has not been made any further complaint. As long as I remain I will take good care that neither on one occasion nor another shall it be revived.'[44]

And two days later (February 10) he wrote again:—

'It is not our business to stir up again the affair of the Downs. If we were to press for an answer, it could be none other than condemnation after so much noise and menaces; silence then must suffice us, as a kind of answer, in place of an open approval, which neither the state of the time or of men's minds permits one to hope.'

Sommelsdijk had judged rightly that his mission, so far as the matter of the Downs was concerned, had achieved all the success that was necessary.

The truth is that Charles, though his pride had been so deeply hurt by the destruction of the Spanish fleet in the presence of an English squadron close to the English shore, was secretly displeased with the Spaniards for having, so to speak, forced his hands in the matter. It was generally assumed at the time, and the statement has frequently been made in histories since, that Charles was aware of the intention of the Spanish admiral to make use of the anchorage at the Downs, should it be necessary for him to seek a place of refuge either from storms or hostile attacks, and that he had previously given permission for him to do so before the fleet left the Spanish harbours. This was not the case. A dispatch[45] from the Secretary of State, Windebank, to Sir Arthur Hopton, the English ambassador at Madrid, dated September 29 (o.s.), that is nearly three weeks after the arrival of Oquendo at the Downs, is conclusive testimony to the contrary. It runs as follows:—

'Your lordship's dispatch of the 3/13 September gives account of a message delivered to you by the Secretary of the Council of War in the King's [Philip IV] name, that he was resolved to put his great fleet to sea for the transportation of his forces to Dunkirk, with intention to chastise the insolences of the French and Hollanders; and thereupon desired his Majesty to afford the fleet a good passage in his seas and accommodations in his harbours, with supplies of the necessary commodities, if it should happen to put into any of them. These letters though they came in extraordinary diligence, yet they arrived not until the fleet had been here in the Downs some days. Now that so great a force of near seventy vessels should put into any of his Majesty's ports, with such numbers of men of war, without his Majesty's leave at all, or so much as his knowledge until they were actually in the ports, besides the neglect and disrespect, is beyond the articles of the peace, and gives occasion enough of jealousy, and would no question be taken highly by them, had his Majesty done the like within their dominions. I am sure it has cast his Majesty into some difficulties and jealousies with the French and Hollanders, and what prejudice it may bring upon his treaties with them is much to be apprehended. It is very true that Don Alonso [the Spanish ambassador, de Cardenas] gave some intimation when his Majesty was in the North that some vessels were preparing in Spain for the transportation of forces into Flanders, and desired his Majesty would not take apprehension at it, but that they might have a friendly reception and treatment in his ports, as occasion should be presented. But he spoke not of so great a number nor such a strength; and it was to be presumed he had meant no other than those English merchant ships that first transported the 1,400 or 1,500 soldiers, and were intercepted and visited by the Hollanders.... When the fleet was come in, notwithstanding they were in distress, having been shrewdly torn and beaten by only seventeen of the Holland ships in their first encounter (a shameful thing, considering the number of the Spanish ships and their vastness, and their ostentation before to chastise both the French and the Hollanders), they refused to do the usual duties by striking to the King's ships; insomuch as Sir John Pennington, our Vice-Admiral, was enforced to threaten to shoot them, if they did it not, and then, after some dispute and much unwillingness, it was yielded to.'

Nothing can be more clear from this whole statement of the situation than the two facts that the Spaniards were not expected, and that they were unwelcome guests.

Why then, it may well be asked, did Charles endure their presence so long in English waters, when it was known that the Dutch were collecting a great fleet in the offing? or why, having endured, did he not take steps to secure his guests from attack by a plain declaration that any breach of neutrality would be treated as a declaration of war and would be resisted by the English admiral? It was because he hoped to be paid for his protection. 'It must be money that must carry the business', wrote Windebank to Hopton. Charles in fact asked for £150,000 sterling, of which £50,000 was to be paid at once; and the Cardinal Infant was busily engaged in obtaining the required sum from the Antwerp money-lenders, when the blow fell and there ceased to be any longer a Spanish fleet to protect. As a striking instance, however, of the diplomatic double-dealing of the times, and one peculiarly characteristic of Stuart policy, it may be mentioned that a dispatch of the French ambassador, Bellievre, dated October 9, testifies to the fact that the Queen was at this very time in the name of the King promising the French Government that, if they would consent to the Palatine prince assuming command of the late Duke Bernhard's army, 'le roi feroit tout ce que nous et les Hollandois pourrons souhaiter en leur faveur contre la flotte d'Espagne, sans néanmoins se déclarer ennemi, en sorte toutefois que les Hollandois auroient lieu d'entreprendre et de faire tout ce que bon leur sembleroit.'[45] Hence the explanation of Pennington's inactivity. Charles was in reality far more angry that Tromp had marred his prospects of striking a good bargain with one or other of the belligerents than at his venturing to infringe a neutrality which was actually in the market. He had not reckoned on the Dutch being able to put so formidable a fleet to sea in so short a time, or bold enough to strike home with such tremendous energy and effect.

Charles, however, should not be altogether blamed for not pursuing at this crisis of his reign a firmer and more consistent policy. Scotland was in rebellion, and he had no funds to raise an army strong enough to restore order. He was face to face with seething disaffection in England. In April, 1640, he found himself compelled, after an interval of ten years, to summon a Parliament in the hopes of obtaining a grant of supplies. Supplies were refused until grievances were amended, and the Short Parliament, as it was called, was dissolved after sitting three weeks. The Long Parliament was to meet in November. It is no wonder that in such circumstances the

King became a pure opportunist in his conduct of foreign policy. His domestic troubles and his financial bankruptcy made it exceedingly difficult for him to steer a straightforward course. The bitter pill of the battle of the Downs had to be swallowed, however disagreeable it might be. It was an accomplished fact, the results of which could not be undone save by war against France and the States, which was in 1640 absolutely impossible. His high pretensions to the sovereignty of the seas, and his claims to demand licences for the fisheries could no longer be insisted upon, his whole interest and attention henceforward were concentrated on the struggle with his own subjects and the maintenance of his sovereign rights within his own Kingdoms.

The proposal therefore for a marriage between the young prince William of Nassau and one of the English princesses was not unwelcome. The Princes of Orange were not of royal rank, but they filled a position of so much dignity and influence in the United Provinces, that it was felt that a union between the families might be advantageous to Charles in securing to him the goodwill of the Dutch in the dangers and difficulties which were thickening round his throne. William was only fifteen years of age, and at first the hand of the younger princess Elizabeth was proposed, that of the Princess Royal being assigned to a Spanish Infant. But Elizabeth was only five years old, the prospect of a Spanish match fell through, and at last in February, 1641, it was arranged that Mary the Princess Royal should be the bride.

The greater part of one of the volumes of the archives of the House of Orange-Nassau, edited by Groen van Prinsterer, is filled with the negotiations concerning this marriage, and the study of the endless notes and dispatches on the subject is replete with interest both for the student of the manners of the times, and because they contain many passages giving lifelike and charming touches concerning the Court of Charles I and Henrietta Maria, and their intimate domestic life. Here it is not possible to treat the subject in greater detail.

The proposed marriage was very popular in England, whose people saw in it the definite adhesion of the King, after many tergiversations, to the Protestant cause. On May 2, Prince William disembarked at Gravesend and proceeded to London in great state to meet his *fiancée*. He was convoyed from Holland by a strong squadron under the command of Admiral Tromp; and was accompanied by the special envoys, Brederode, Aerssen van Sommelsdijk, Heenvliet, and the resident ambassador, Joachimi. In their report to the Stadholder of the reception (May 2, 1641), the envoys write:

'We had to pass through so many people, it was almost impossible to reach the Court, except for the good order which was kept from street to street. Your Highness could not imagine with what blessings and acclamations his Highness was received, and we would venture to say that not for a century has a reception taken place in which great and small have testified so much joy and satisfaction.'

It was to be the last glimmer of brightness in the life of Charles and Henrietta Maria. The boy and girl, aged respectively fifteen and ten years, were married in state on May 12, 1641, in the chapel at Whitehall—a marriage destined to sorrow, but which was to have such important results upon the future relations of England and the United Provinces. Nine years later William was suddenly cut off by an attack of small-pox in the midst of a promising career. A week after his death Mary gave birth to a son, who was to be famous in history as William III, Prince of Orange and King of England.

VI: 1641-1653

The marriage of the Princess Royal with the son of Frederick Henry, Prince of Orange, on May 12, 1641, took place at an ominous time. Ten days later Strafford was executed. There can be little or no doubt, that the eagerness of the King and Queen for the accomplishment of this union was due to the desire to secure the goodwill of the Stadholder, and through him of the States, in the troublous times which they saw before them. It fulfilled two objects. It gave satisfaction to the Puritan party in England as being a Protestant alliance, and it was accompanied by secret assurances on the part of Frederick Henry of friendly support to the King in his coming conflict with his subjects. These assurances, we may well believe, were very guarded and strictly personal, for no one knew better than the Stadholder the limitations of his actual power. The following passage from a letter in the hand of Sommelsdijk, written March 5 in the name of the envoys to Frederick Henry, puts the matter very clearly:

'We have found so much frankness and affection on the part of the King and Queen for the furtherance of the marriage, that we have no fear in recommending your Highness to hasten the departure of Monseigneur the Prince your son, as much as possible, so as to put everything in security; for their Majesties have resolved to push forward without allowing themselves to be stopped by any machinations to the contrary from whatever part they come, and whatever they write to you, upon the good faith and confidence of Mr. de Heenvliet, remains secret without anything of it escaping either here or there, for fear lest the cognizance of it should come to the knowledge of the Parliament.'[14]

William returned to Holland at the end of May alone, leaving his child-bride for awhile in her parents' home. But the Grand Remonstrance, the impeachment of the five members, and other events now followed in rapid succession, and soon it was seen that the issues which divided King and Parliament admitted of no accommodation by peaceful means. Heenvliet, who was still in England, became the trusted confidant of the distracted King and Queen, and his letters to Frederick Henry at this time show how anxious Charles was to avoid a civil war, if by any concessions that did not utterly despoil him—'le dèpouiller tout-à-fait'—he could come to terms with the Parliament. In private interviews Henrietta Maria was urgent with Heenvliet to use his good offices, and many times expressed the hope that should matters come to an extremity 'the Prince would not allow the King to perish'. In reply the Stadholder impressed upon their Majesties not to have recourse to arms, for victory was uncertain. A reconciliation on whatever terms could not but be to the profit and advantage of the King. Unfortunately such advice was already too late to be of any avail (February, 1642).

At the beginning of March Henrietta Maria accompanied the Princess Royal to Holland. Her real object was to collect funds and to secure, if possible, the active assistance of the Prince of Orange. She was received with much distinction and magnificence, but her thoughts were not upon the shows of state. Letter upon letter passed from her to the Stadholder in his camp, begging him to help her in procuring supplies of money, arms, men, and munitions of war for her husband's service. She tried to borrow upon her jewels, but the Jews would give her nothing without the guarantee of the Prince. Lords Jermyn and Digby hurried backwards and forwards upon her confidential missions, and she had many interviews with Heenvliet, with whom she had become so intimate during his sojourn in London. What a picture of the feverish state of anxiety to which her troubles had brought the once gay and buoyant Henrietta Maria, is contained in a report of one of her conversations with him sent by Heenvliet to the Prince of Orange.

'I confess that this interview has troubled me not a little. The Queen did not speak to me on the subject without trembling, and she kept asking me so piteously, if there were not any hope that by any means your Highness could be persuaded to assist her, that I am still troubled at it.'

Frederick Henry did his very best to give all the help he could, both in his private and official capacity. He allowed the English officers serving in his army to return home and join the King's forces, where their services were of great value. He gave the guarantee she required for a loan upon the Crown jewels, he advanced a considerable sum of money out of his private purse, and he connived at arms and ammunition being secretly bought and sent to England from Dutch ports; but he was unable to promise any assistance from the States, nor indeed could he venture even to suggest it. The bulk of the Dutch people in the opening stages of the Civil War took the side of the Parliament, more especially the Hollanders. The Prince's influence could still command the support of a majority in the States-General, but he, like all the Stadholders of his House, had constantly to struggle with the opposition of the aristocratic burgher-regents of the towns of Holland, who controlled the States of that dominant province. Maurice had crushed by force in 1618 the attempt of Oldenbarneveldt to claim for each province of the Union independent sovereign rights, but the spirit of Oldenbarneveldt survived, and the Hollanders, conscious of the power of the purse that they possessed, were ready to thwart the plans and policy of the Stadholders, though these were supported by the other provinces, and indeed did thwart them by raising difficulties in the way of obtaining supplies. Frederick Henry, during the first decade of his Stadholderate, exercised a larger personal authority in the direction of the affairs of the Republic than any of his predecessors or successors. But during the last years of his life, prematurely worn out by constant campaigning, he had continually to confront the bitter opposition of the town corporations of Holland to that vigorous prosecution of the war that he desired. The Prince of Orange then was not his own master, and could not in face of the strong leanings of a large part of the population, in Holland particularly, towards the Parliamentary cause in the Civil War give effect to his own inclination to lend the King active support in his efforts to suppress rebellion by armed force.

Matters came to a crisis when, at the end of August, a special envoy from the Parliament, Walter Strickland, appeared at the Hague with instructions to protest against the dispatch of warlike stores to the King from Dutch ports, and the permitting of officers in the Dutch service to join his army. The Queen was highly indignant. The English resident ambassador, Boswell, at her bidding immediately presented himself before the States-General to protest and demand that Strickland should not be received or acknowledged. To the Prince she wrote, September 6, 1642, begging him to prevent such an affront being offered to the King, 'for assuredly', to quote her actual words, 'it would be so great, that he could never have any friendship with these States after this; and, God be thanked, he is not yet in such a state as to be despised.' But although the majority of the States-General were ready to refuse Strickland any audience, they were forced by the insistance of the States of Holland to make a compromise. They would not admit him to the assembly of the States-General, but they agreed to send two deputies to confer with him. The result was, again by the pressure of Holland, that the States-General declared for strict neutrality, and forbade the export to either side in the Civil War of arms or munitions of war. Despite this prohibition, by the connivance of the Stadholder, friends of the royal cause contrived to dispatch ammunition and other stores to Dunkirk, and from thence to ship it to England. Strickland, having heard of this, ventured to make a written complaint to the States-General of the Prince's conduct. Frederick Henry thereupon declared that such an aspersion was an insult to his person and demanded satisfaction. The States-General, May 7, 1643, declared thereupon the accusation of Strickland to be false, and broke off all relations with him.

Henrietta Maria had returned to England the previous February, never ceasing to the end her tireless efforts on her husband's behalf. Before leaving she had broached the project of a second alliance between the families, that of the Prince of Wales with the eldest daughter of the Stadholder. It was not a mere ephemeral project, for the following year a certain Dr. Goff, who had been chaplain to one of the English regiments in the Dutch service, was sent over by the Queen, with a letter in which she says 'from me you will only know that the King my lord has given me full and authentic powers to negotiate and to conclude the marriage of my son the Prince of Wales with Mademoiselle d'Orange.' With these powers Dr. Goff was entrusted. In his instructions were contained the onerous conditions, which must be the price paid for the honour of such a match. The States were to break with France unless the latter would consent to give armed assistance to the King, or in default of this to make peace with Spain, one of the conditions of such a peace being a promise of help to Charles. It is needless to say that the proposal was not acceptable, for the simple reason that Frederick Henry had no power to comply with the conditions, even if he had wished. The negotiations, however, went on all through 1645, although the desperate state of the King's affairs after the battle of Naseby rendered any successful issue impossible. Louise of Nassau became shortly afterwards the wife of the Great Elector.

In 1644 two envoys, William Boreel and Jan van Rheede, were sent to England to attempt to mediate between the King and the Parliament. Their instructions, containing fifty-seven articles, are dated October 6, 1643, but they did not actually set out until January 15 following. They had interviews with Lord Denbigh, Sir Harry Mildemay, and Sir William Strickland, representing the Parliament, and afterwards, February 19, an audience with the King in the hall of Christ Church at Oxford. During the whole of the year 1644 they remained in England, and took part in the abortive negotiations of Uxbridge, which came to an end February 22, 1645. It became now evident to the ambassadors that they could do no further good, more especially as the Parliament more and more showed a disinclination to accept foreign mediation. After farewell audiences they reached the Hague again, May 4, 1645, and made their report to the States-General. It was unfavourable to the attitude of the Parliament. On being informed of this by their representative, Strickland, who was again at the Hague, the Parliament requested him to appear before the States-General and offer a justification on their behalf in reply to Boreel and Van Rheede. The States-General, by the votes of Utrecht, Groningen, Zeeland, and Overyssel against Holland, Gelderland, and Friesland, refused him admission, while at the same time they permitted the King's resident, Boswell, to appear in their assembly and address them. The Parliament on this had their justification printed in English and Dutch, and secretly distributed throughout the Provinces. It was eagerly read, the mass of the people being in favour of what they regarded as the cause of civil and religious freedom against despotic rule, especially as there were many points of resemblance between the struggle in England and their own long drawn out struggle against Spanish tyranny. This marked division of opinion in the Netherlands effactually prevented any further steps being taken to interfere in English affairs during the two next years.

Events, however, had been moving fast during that interval. On March 14, 1647, Frederick Henry died. At the very end of his life he had deserted the French alliance, of which he had so long been a strong advocate, and had joined his great influence to that of the Province of Holland in bringing about a separate peace with Spain. With the increasing growth of the military strength of France, the project of a division of the Spanish Netherlands with that power ceased to have attractions for him. At the time of his death all the conditions of peace with Spain had been practically settled, the terms being virtually those dictated by the Dutch. By the treaty which was actually signed at Munster, January 30, 1648, Spain, after eighty years of strife, was at last compelled to recognize the independence of the United Provinces, and all the conquests made by Frederick Henry in Flanders, Brabant, and Limburg remained in the hands of the Dutch, as prizes of war. At this proud moment in commerce, in seaborne trade, in finance, in colonial expansion and enterprise, in arts and in letters, the Dutch Republic had reached the zenith of its prosperity. The Civil War in England had paralysed the energies of its chief rival upon the seas, and left the way clear for the United Provinces to step into the very first rank of maritime powers.

Frederick Henry was succeeded in his posts and dignities by his son. William II, Prince of Orange, had only reached his twenty-second year at the time of his father's death, but he was full of talent and energy, fired with ambition, eager to emulate the great deeds of his ancestors, and, if possible, to excel them. His wife, Mary of England, was still a girl. Haughty in manner, and exceedingly tenacious of her royal rank, she preferred always to be styled the Princess Royal, rather than Princess of Orange. The relations between the youthful pair were, however, thoroughly sympathetic, and William was ever ready to lend a helping hand to his English relations and never made any secret of his zeal in their cause. His hospitality to them was unbounded, and his purse open. First, the Duke of York made his escape from England to Holland, April, 1648, and he was followed by the Prince of Wales in July. As the Queen of Bohemia was still residing at the Hague with her daughters, quite a family party were assembled at the Court of William and Mary. The Prince of Wales, who was courteously received by a deputation of the States-General, found a loyal squadron assembled at Hellevoetsluys, of which he assumed command. He also raised some troops for his service in the islands of Borkum and Juist. There was at one time danger of a collision in Dutch waters between the royal ships and a Parliamentary squadron under the Earl of Warwick. The Parliament dispatched an envoy, Dr. Doreslaar, a native of Enkhuysen, who had settled in England and had become Professor of History at Cambridge, to protest against the protection and assistance accorded to the royalists. The States-General refused to grant him an audience. Towards the close of the year, Walter Strickland was again sent to the Hague, furnished with fresh credentials, to join Dr. Doreslaar and demand in the name of the Parliament that the royal fleet should not be furnished with arms and stores in Dutch harbours. He was escorted by Lord Warwick, with a fleet of twenty-one ships. The States-General took steps to prevent a hostile encounter between the rival fleets, but could not be moved even to give a hearing to the Parliament's request. The States of Holland, however, received Doreslaar, and passed a resolution forbidding the royal ships and stores to remain in the harbours of that province.

The news of the impending trial of Charles I for high-treason caused consternation in the States, and especially in Orangist circles. The Prince of Wales himself, who had now handed over the command of his fleet to Prince Rupert and was residing with his brother-in-law at the Hague, appeared in person before the States-General to ask them to intercede for his father. All parties concurred in granting his request, and it was unanimously resolved that an extraordinary embassy should be sent to London, and in order to strip it of any appearance of partisanship, the chosen envoy was not an Orangist, but Adrian Pauw, lord of Heemstede, the veteran leader of the Aristocratic-Hollander party. With him was associated Albert Joachimi, who through the whole of the Civil War had remained at his post, as resident ambassador in London. Besides his credentials, Pauw carried with him letters for Fairfax, Cromwell, and other Parliamentary leaders. The embassy was received with courtesy Feb. 5/Jan. 26, 1649, and Pauw pressed for an immediate audience. It was too late. On the following day the death sentence was pronounced. The envoys now approached, Sunday, Feb. 7/Jan. 28, Fairfax, Cromwell, and others privately, asking for a respite of the sentence, but failed to get any definite answer. On the Monday they were granted an audience at a special sitting of the House of Commons, and in the name of the States-General, Pauw and Joachimi read an address interceding for the King's life, and setting out the reasons for the course for which they were pleading. A general answer was given, that what they had said should be considered. In reality the decision had already been taken for the public execution of the King the next morning, Tuesday, Feb. 9/Jan. 30. The ambassadors had their address translated from French into English, and on seeing the preparations in Whitehall, again made an effort to obtain an immediate audience, but they found the way barred by troops, and knew that the object of their mission could no longer be achieved.

Not till February 25/15 was an official answer given to Pauw and Joachimi, in which, after thanking the States for their friendly intentions, the Parliament declined to discuss the question of the King's execution. But at the same time an earnest desire was expressed for the establishment of a firm peace, a right understanding and good correspondence between the governments of the two countries, which had so many common interests. 'We shall', they said, 'be ever ready not only to hear but to contribute with them all good means and offices to fulfil such works as shall be necessary for the general good of Christendom, as well as our own.' There can be no doubt that Cromwell's influence may be seen in this friendly overture. Cromwell had already given Pauw an assurance in a private interview of his wish for the establishment of close relations of friendship with the Dutch, and had spoken of a proposal being made for giving the Netherlanders the same commercial privileges in England as the inhabitants of the country. Already there was floating before his eyes that idea, which he was afterwards in a position to try and realize, of effecting such a close union between the two republics as would make them into one State.

In 1649 any thought of such a thing was a mere dream. The news of the King's execution caused a wave of horror and indignation to sweep over the Netherlands without distinction of class or party. The States-General decided unanimously to offer their condolences to the Prince of Wales and also to congratulate him on his accession. The Orangists would have liked his full title to have been given to him of King of Great Britain and Ireland, but the States of Holland and Zeeland, who were the most interested in trade and shipping, opposed this, as they were afraid of the resentment of the new government in England. So it was agreed that he should be addressed simply as King Charles II. To this title he had an undoubted right, as he had been proclaimed king in Scotland on his father's death. The States of Holland separately also sent a deputation to him for the same purpose. The number of broadsheets and pamphlets that issued from the press are a proof of how deeply moved the whole country was at the tragic death of the English King. What was most remarkable was the fact recorded by Clarendon[*] as to the change of attitude among the preachers, who had hitherto been strongly on the side of the Parliament. 'The body of the clergy', he writes, 'in a Latin oration delivered by the chief preacher of the Hague, lamented the misfortune in terms of as much asperity, and detestation of the actors, as unworthy the name of Christians, as could be expressed.' Nevertheless, in order to avoid an open breach with the Commonwealth, as it was now styled, Joachimi was allowed to remain, as the States' resident ambassador in London.

The English Council of State, on their part, determined to send over once more Dr. Isaac Doreslaar to join Strickland at the Hague, with instructions to propose to the States-General the knitting together in closer relations of the common interests of the two countries. He arrived May 9. Doreslaar was especially hateful to the royalists, who were gathered at that time in large numbers in the Dutch capital, as he had taken part in the King's trial, and rumour had even designated him as the masked headsman. It was an unhappy choice, which had serious consequences. Three days after his arrival, Doreslaar, as he sat at table in his hotel, was attacked by five or six men, and assassinated. The assassins, their work accomplished, walked off undisturbed. The body was sent back to England, and was honoured with a public interment in Westminster Abbey. 'Though all who were engaged in this enterprise', writes Clarendon, 'went quietly away, and so out of the town, insomuch as no one of them was ever apprehended or called in question, yet they kept not their own counsel so well (believing they had done a very heroic act) but that it was generally known that they were all Scottish men, and most of them servants or dependents upon the Marquis of Montrose.'

The States of Holland, as soon as news reached them of what had happened, made great efforts to track the murderers, but in vain, and Joachimi was commissioned to express their horror at the act, and to try and appease the Parliament. The Parliament, on their side, did not feel themselves sufficiently secure to take decisive action, and Strickland was instructed to approach the States-General once more with offers of friendship. But the influence of the Prince of Orange in the States-General was paramount, and Strickland was refused an audience. On the other hand, despite Strickland's protest, the Scottish envoy, Macdowell, sent by Charles II to announce his accession to the throne of the northern kingdom, was received by them. The English Council of State were unable to regard this conduct in any other light than as a deliberate insult to them and their representative. Strickland was recalled, and Joachimi was informed that unless he was provided with fresh letters of credit to the Republican Government within a fixed time he must leave the land. Strickland left Holland, July 22, 1650. Joachimi received orders to quit London, September 26. All this time the States of Holland had been doing their utmost to effect an accommodation. The trade interests of the province with England were so great that they were most anxious to avoid a breach with the new Commonwealth. They on their own authority received Strickland in a public audience, and even ventured so far as to send a commissary, Gerard Schaep by name, to London, January 22. This high-handed act of independence only had the effect, however, of stiffening the backs of the States-General. All the efforts of Holland to change their attitude towards England failed.

The acute differences of view in regard to this particular line of policy between the self-willed province and the Stadholder were but the signs of a general estrangement; and the struggle for predominance was destined to come to a head at the very time of the return of Joachimi. The Prince of Orange had been altogether opposed to the abandonment of the French alliance and the conclusion of a separate treaty with Spain in 1648. The peace of Munster had carried into effect the policy of the States of Holland, and William II was determined, as soon as he got the reins of power firmly into his hands, to reverse it. He entered into secret negotiations with Mazarin for a renewal of a French alliance against Spain, with the aim of conquering and partitioning the Spanish Netherlands. Devotedly attached to the Stuart cause, it was his intention with French help to try to overthrow the English Commonwealth and establish Charles II on his father's throne. His generosity to his wife's exiled relations was so great that he impoverished himself and had to raise large loans on his estates. With ambitious schemes of war and conquest filling his brain, he found himself speedily in disagreement with the merchant burghers of the Province of Holland. The chief interest of the Hollanders was peace, which would reduce taxation and increase commerce. They had long grudged the heavy charges of the war, and the Provincial States, as soon as peace was concluded, clamoured for the disbanding of a large number of the regiments, which, though they formed part of the federal army, were in the pay of the Province of Holland. William, as Captain-General of the Union, opposed this, and was supported by the States-General. Into the details of this contest for supremacy it is needless to enter here. It was to a certain extent a repetition of that between Maurice and Oldenbarneveldt. Armed with the authority of the States-General, William in the summer of 1650, at the head of a strong body of troops, forced the States of Holland to submission. In the previous year Charles, on his departure for Scotland, had begged the support of the States-General, and had promised in return to settle favourably the long-standing differences about Amboina and Pulo Run in the East Indies, and other questions, but owing to the opposition of Holland and Zeeland no active assistance was given. The States-General, however, as a mark of sympathy and goodwill, assembled in a body to bid him farewell. The royal cause had at first prospered in Scotland, until September 13/3, 1650, when the battle of Dunbar shattered Charles's fair prospects. But at this very time his brother-in-law had just brought his contest with the Province of Holland to a triumphant issue. William II was now in a position to bring about that active intervention of the States in alliance with France in support of the Stuart cause, and for the expulsion of the

Spaniards from the Southern Netherlands, on which his heart was set. To the Prince of Orange therefore the eyes of the English royalist party were turned, as their chief hope in the hour when it seemed as if nothing could stem the tide of Cromwell's victories. They were doomed to a terrible disappointment. William, in the very midst of secret negotiations with France, suddenly fell sick of the small-pox, and after a week's illness died, November 6, 1650. He was but twenty-four, and in him Charles II lost a chivalrous and true-hearted friend. Eager for fame, gifted with uncommon abilities, William, had he lived, was undoubtedly prepared to have put his far-reaching plans into execution, and to have risked much for the upholding of his kinsman's rights.

His decease brought about a revolution in the United Provinces. He left no one of his family to take his place. His only child was not born until a week after his death. The Province of Holland straightway seized the opportunity to assert that predominance in the Union for which it had been striving so long. Its leaders at once took steps to call an extraordinary assembly, known as the 'Great Gathering', to take into consideration the state of the Union, of religion, and military affairs. The Great Gathering met at the Hague, January 18, 1651. The office of Stadholder was abolished, in all the provinces but Friesland, as were also the posts of Captain-General and Admiral-General of the Union. The population and the wealth of Holland gave henceforth to the States of that province a position of supremacy in the federation, and, as in the days of Oldenbarneveldt, all the threads of administration and the conduct of foreign affairs passed during the Stadholderless period into the hands of its chief functionary, the *Raad-Pensionaris* or Grand Pensionary.

This complete change in the system of government of the United Provinces caused much satisfaction in London. The aristocratic burgher oligarchy, who were now in power at the Hague, had no special sympathy for Charles II. Indeed it was embittered against him at this time, since Prince Rupert's ships from their head-quarters in the Scilly Islands had been plundering Dutch merchantmen in their passage up channel. The Parliament therefore determined to send a special embassy to propose that close alliance between the two neighbouring republics, almost amounting to a political union, which Cromwell had already set before him as an end to be aimed at for the mutual advantage of both States. The States-General on their side had, on the proposal of the States of Holland, determined, January 28, 1651, to recognize the English Commonwealth as a free republic, and to receive its envoys, and Joachimi again went to London to take up his old post as the resident ambassador of the States.

The English ambassadors were Oliver St. John and Walter Strickland, the latter of whom, as we have seen, had spent many years in Holland without being able to obtain an audience with the States-General. The Parliament were now determined that their representatives should make their state entry into the Hague with a splendour befitting the envoys of so mighty a power. They were accompanied by a suite of some 250 persons in brilliant uniforms and liveries, and travelled in twenty-five state coaches.

On March 27, 1651, the solemn entry took place. The ambassadors were, however, to pass through the ordeal of an unpleasant experience. As the procession made its way through the crowded streets, St. John and Strickland were greeted with loud cries of 'Regicides', 'Executioners', 'Cromwell's bastards', and other abusive epithets. No doubt there were many royalist refugees in the Hague, but though these may have given the lead to the mob, there can be little question of the general hostility at this time of the masses of the people, even in Holland itself, to the Parliament. It is a common mistake to suppose that the Orangist was the aristocratic, the republican, or so-called 'States' party, the popular party in the United Provinces. The States of Holland, which was the stronghold of the republican party, was entirely in the hands of the close oligarchic corporations of the chief towns of the province. In each town a few aristocratic burgher families monopolized all offices and authority, the rest of the townsmen had no votes or representation, and the country people were ignored altogether. The great influence and executive powers of the Stadholders of the house of Orange were therefore a check upon the domination of these burgher oligarchies, and so by them resented accordingly. On the other hand, the Princes of Orange were loved and respected by the people, alike for their high qualities and the great services they had rendered to the country, and there was scarcely any time when they had not the enthusiastic support of the great majority of those classes, the bulk of the population, who were excluded from any share in the government of the State. A knowledge of these facts is absolutely necessary to a right understanding of what the 'Stadholderless' régime in the time of John de Witt really meant.

The parliamentary ambassadors were really alarmed, remembering the fate of Doreslaar, at this hostile reception. Neither they nor their attendants dared to venture into the streets but in parties of five or six and sword in hand; and everywhere they were followed by the cry of 'Regicides'. On March 29, St. John and Strickland presented their credentials before the 'Great Gathering', and in a long speech expressed the desire of the English Government for the establishment of good relations of enduring friendship between the two republics. 'It is the wish of the Parliament to conclude', they said, 'a closer union of the two States, which would be for both more advantageous than heretofore, since it would not be dependent upon the life and will and private interests of a single individual.' Six commissioners were appointed by the Assembly to discuss their proposals, and a conference was opened on April 4. The grounds on which the English proposed to the Netherlanders that 'a more strict and intimate Alliance and Union bee entred into by them, whereby there may bee a more intrinsecall and mutual interest of each other, than hath hitherto beene for the good of both', were: (1) community of religion, (2) community of political liberty, (3) community of interest in freedom of trade and navigation. The Dutch, however, showed themselves very wary. They had no intention of giving their consent to any general propositions before informing themselves of their precise meaning. There was considerable variety of opinion in the different provinces and much indecision. On April 6, the commissioners were only empowered to reply, that the States were willing 'not only to renew the ancient friendship between the two nations, but also to conclude a treaty for common interests'. This response did not satisfy the English envoys, who rejoined that 'the union for common interests' they had in view 'was one closer than at any previous time'. These words required explanation, but it seemed that they could only point to an alliance so intimate and binding as to be another term for coalition. Such was indeed its meaning in the minds of those who proposed it, and so the Dutch interpreted it. To them, however, not unnaturally, the only idea suggested by a coalition with the English Commonwealth was the loss by the smaller republic of its independence, and its practical absorption in the larger. Such an idea was simply unthinkable to men who had just won the recognition of their independence after eighty years of heroic struggle. The reply of the Assembly was not hurriedly given. At last, on April 26, it came, and was so far unsatisfactory that, while expressing their readiness for a closer union, the reservation was made that it must be one 'in which both States could better promote their interests for themselves and for the common welfare'. St. John and Strickland now went a step further, and gave a hint that if an offensive and defensive confederation such as they had in mind could be accomplished, it would be accompanied by many advantageous concessions to the Dutch. At this point the negotiations came to an end. The Parliament did not believe that in the present temper of the Dutch their proposals were likely to be received in the spirit in which they were offered, and the ambassadors were recalled. They and their attendants were constantly insulted by Royalists and Orangists whenever they showed themselves out of doors, and though the provincial authorities strictly forbade such outrages on pain of severe penalties, and urged the citizens to assist in the protection of the representatives of a foreign power, they effected little. Some of the offenders were of high rank[48], and they openly braved the threats of the magistracy and remained unpunished. Earnest representations were now made to the English Parliament on behalf of the States of Holland by their agent, Gerard Schaep, who was still residing in London, that they would allow the envoys of the Commonwealth to remain awhile longer and continue the negotiations. The Parliament, however, would only consent to do this on condition that full satisfaction be made to St. John and Strickland for all that they had endured, and that the attacks upon them should cease. The States of Holland promised to do this. Prince Edward of the Palatine and other prominent offenders were summoned before a court of justice, and warned; some of their servants were punished. It was a sorry piece of business. But it was an index to the real feeling of the populace that such a state of things should have been possible in a town like the Hague.

The negotiations were accordingly renewed by the presentation of fresh proposals, May 10, by St. John and Strickland. There was now no mention of coalition, only of an offensive and defensive alliance, but there was an ominous addition: both States were required to bind themselves severally not to permit the sojourn on their soil of declared enemies of the other. This was especially directed against the adherents of the Stuarts and the members of the Orange and Palatinate families. The great desire of the party now in power in the Netherlands was the maintenance of peace. The Hollanders were willing to conclude a treaty extending their trade privileges, but they were anxious not to be drawn into the war in Scotland, and in face of the popular affection for the house of Orange they dared not venture at the dictation of a foreign power to treat the young prince and his mother harshly. They responded therefore, after some delay, by counter proposals for the renewal of the Treaty of 1496, the *Magnus Intercursus*, but revised in favour of the Dutch to suit present-day conditions. Complete freedom of trade, navigation, and fishery without pass, toll, or other hindrances in each other's domains was what was aimed at. No mention was made of the English proposal to banish from the Netherlands those who gave help to the Stuart cause. With such differences of view there was of course no prospect of any agreement being reached. The English embassy accordingly left the Hague, July 31, 1651, and returned home.

The report made to Parliament created a bad impression in England, and led to all the old complaints against the Dutch being raked up once more: the massacre of Amboina, the seizure of Pulo Run and other high-handed acts in the East Indies, their monopoly of the fisheries on the British coasts, their attacks on the English whalers off Spitzbergen, and their attempts to drive out English trade from the Baltic, from Russia, and elsewhere. Then on the top of this the shameful treatment to which the parliamentary envoys had been persistently exposed was angrily recalled, the refusal of the States-General for years to admit Strickland to an audience, the murder of Doreslaar, and lastly the insults offered to the latest embassy. All these things formed a formidable bill of indictment. As the efforts of the Parliament to effect a close union between the republics for their common interest had failed, it became the clear duty of the English Government to take measures to protect the national interests against unscrupulous rivals. There was no delay in taking drastic action.

On October 9, 1651, the famous Navigation Act was passed, which forbade the importation of foreign goods and products into English harbours save in English bottoms, or those of the countries from whence the goods and products came. A deadly blow was thus struck at the Netherlanders, who had at that time almost a monopoly of the most important branches of sea-borne trade and were the carriers of the world. Scarcely less serious was the prohibition to foreigners to fish in British waters. Every infringement of this edict would be punished by the confiscation of the offending vessels. It has already been seen in previous lectures of what vital importance these fisheries were to the welfare of Holland.

The States-General now determined to make a serious effort to resume the negotiations which had been broken off, and Jacob Cats, Gerard Schaep, and Paulus van der Perre were sent on a special embassy to England. They reached London,

December 27. Their task was a difficult one. They pressed for the revocation of the Navigation Act and of the embargo upon fishing, and for the release of the confiscated ships, and proposed that negotiations should again be set on foot for the conclusion of a treaty based upon the *Magnus Intercursus*. The news at this critical moment that the Dutch were fitting out 150 new war vessels for the protection of free navigation did not tend to smooth the way to an understanding. It was regarded in England as a threat. The English now formulated their demands. These were such as they must have known would never be conceded. They required the payment of the arrears of toll due for the fishing on the British coasts, the surrender of the Spice Islands, the punishment of the survivors of those concerned in the Amboina massacre, satisfaction for the murder of Doreslaar, and the payment of the indemnities due for losses sustained by Englishmen at the hands of the Dutch in various parts of the world. It is clear that these demands were practically an ultimatum. The Netherlanders were required to choose between coalition or humiliation, and in case neither were accepted, war. Both sides were, however, averse to taking the final step, and conferences and negotiations still dragged on for some months, while strenuous preparations were at the same time being made on both sides of the Channel for hostilities. It was a dangerous situation, and was made wellnigh desperate by a conflict which took place off Folkestone, May 19, 1652, between the Dutch fleet under Tromp and an English squadron under Blake, through a misunderstanding about the question of striking the flag. This event excited public opinion in England to fever pitch, and made war practically inevitable. The Dutch Government, however, knew that they were not prepared for such a mighty conflict. The peace party in Holland had insisted on the disbanding of a large part of the land forces after the death of William, and the navy had been neglected and was far from being as formidable as a few years before. In all haste therefore the experienced Adrian Pauw, now holding the important post of Grand Pensionary of Holland, was sent over to London to join Cats, Schaep, and van Perre, and endeavour even at the last moment to avoid a final breach between the two nations. His efforts proved vain, for the English would not give way in their demands for conditions too humiliating for the Netherlanders to accept. The 'States' party in power had, in fact, not a free hand, even had they been inclined to preserve peace at the cost of submission to English dictation, for the Orangists were delighted at the thought of trying conclusions with the hated Commonwealth, and they had strong support throughout the country. The fear of a revolution compelled the States-General to refuse the only terms by which war could be avoided. The die was cast. The Dutch ambassadors left England, June 30, and the struggle between the two maritime powers for supremacy, which had been so frequently imminent but so long delayed, at last began.

APPENDIX

A. THE GREAT OR HERRING FISHERY.

From the nature of the land, Holland and Zeeland were always the home of fisher-folk. The herring fishery off the coast of Great Britain was from early times an industry pursued by many Hollanders and Zeelanders, but it was comparatively limited, until the invention of 'curing' made by Willem Beukelsz of Biervliet in the latter part of the fourteenth century (he probably died in 1397) converted a perishable article of food into a commercial commodity. The method of Beukelsz, which remained practically unchanged for some five centuries, without going into minute particulars, consisted in the following processes. Immediately after the hauling in of the nets the guts were in a particular manner removed from the fish, which were then packed in layers in barrels with salt between the layers. In the brine or pickle that was formed they were allowed to lie some time, fresh salt being added every fortnight. At first the Zeelanders were the chief herring fishers, but afterwards the towns on the Zuyder Zee and on the Maas became the head-quarters of the industry. During the Burgundian period many laws were enacted regulating the herring fisheries, but the edict[49] of Charles V, May 18, 1519, which extended and codified all previous enactments, remained the permanent basis of future legislation on the subject. The chief regulations concerned the branding of the barrels, the sorting of the fish, and the date of the beginning of the fishing. This date was originally August 24 (St. Bartholomew), but was afterwards changed first to July 25 (St. James), and finally to June 24 (St. John the Baptist). It is possible that some change in the habits of the herring shoals may have led to this considerable shifting of the date. After 1519 there were many fresh enactments made, referring particularly to matters concerning convoys and their cost, the duties levied, and many details in regard to the boats, tackle, and crews, and again a codification of all laws was carried out by a series of edicts in 1580, 1582, and 1584. These edicts of 1580 and 1582 (Groot Placaetboek van Holland en West Vriesland, tom i., 684-691, 696-707, 715-727, 748-751), continued to regulate the fisheries during the period with which these lectures deal; i.e. the first half of the seventeenth century. Especial attention was given in these regulations to the branding of the barrels in which the herrings were packed. Each fishing town had its official inspectors, who themselves branded the barrels with the mark of the cooper and that of the town, and no others were allowed to be used. The kind of salt for the curing was rigorously prescribed, and careful precautions taken that no other kind or damaged salt was smuggled on board. Not less minute were the regulations to ensure that the quality of the fish which came to the market should be guaranteed. All fish had to be sorted. Such as were caught before July 25 (St. James), being not fully developed, had to be kept apart. Such as were caught after July 25 had to be divided according to technical categories, 'full and sweet', 'empty', 'undersized or damaged'; and the skipper was enjoined under oath to place his own mark upon each barrel and to be personally responsible for the quality assigned, and not only so, the fisherman who packed the fish in the barrel was required to place his mark upon it. The most stringent rules were laid down as the correct method of curing. In fact, everything was done to show the importance of the industry, and the necessity of securing that the market was supplied with no counterfeit article, but only with herrings prepared in Dutch fashion by Dutch hands. In order to keep a fast hold upon the monopoly, the fishermen were forbidden under heavy penalties to sell their fish in foreign ports. In the seventeenth century, the interests of those engaged in this profitable trade were vigilantly looked after by a body known as the 'College of the Great Fishery', which met at Delft. The College consisted of five deputies from the towns of Enkhuysen, Schiedam, Delft, Rotterdam, and Brill, and so exclusive were they that during the period with which we are concerned other towns, even such important places as Amsterdam, Dordrecht, and Hoorn, were refused admission. One of the chief tasks of the College was to enforce the carrying out of the regulations.

During the reigns of the two first Stuarts, the Dutch fishing fleet was accustomed to sail out for the Scottish waters between the Shetlands and Cape Buchan Ness in the middle of June, so as to begin their fishing operations on St. John's Day, June 24. From June 24 to July 25, the fishing was wholly in the north; from July 25 to September 14 to the south of Buchan Ness, but still along the Scottish coast; from September 25 to November 25 in the neighbourhood of Yarmouth; from November 25 to January 31 off the mouth of the Thames and the Kentish coast. The fleet sailed out twice only, in June and again in the autumn, the task of conveying the barrels of fish from the fishing 'busses' to the Dutch harbours being carried out by a number of light vessels called 'ventjagers.' The herring fleet was always accompanied by an armed convoy, to the upkeep of which the State contributed 20,000 florins annually. In war time a small naval squadron was also detached to keep watch and ward against the attacks of Spanish cruisers and Dunkirk pirates.

The Herring or Great Fishery was compulsorily closed on January 31. During the spring months the fishermen occupied themselves with fishing by hook on the Dogger Bank, for cod, soles, and other fish. This was named 'The Small Fishery'.

B. THE NARROW SEAS.

The expression 'the Narrow Sea', or 'the Narrow Seas', which so often appears in seventeenth-century diplomatic dispatches and controversial writings, is a term upon whose exact signification geographically there has been much dispute. The English kings from ancient times claimed 'sovereignty'—*dominium maris*—in the 'narrow seas' or *mare britannicum*. Evidence is fairly conclusive that the term under the Tudors and until the friction with the Dutch arose on the questions of free fishery and the striking of the flag in the reign of James I, was confined to the Channel, the narrow sea between England and France. Lord Salisbury, as late as 1609, writing to Sir R. Winwood at the Hague (Winwood, *Mem.* iii, p. 50), speaks of 'his Majesty's narrow seas between England and France, where the whole appertayneth to him in right, and hath been possessed tyme out of mind by his progenitors.' It soon, however, became the accepted interpretation of English statesmen, jurists, and writers that the 'narrow seas' meant the two seas between England and France, and England and the Netherlands; thus Rapin (*Hist. d'Angleterre* vii, p. 454), 'la domination des deux Mers, c'est-à-dire, des deux bras de Mer qui se trouvent entre l'Angleterre et la France et entre l'Allemagne et la Grande-Bretagne.' This extension of the term was vigorously contested by the Dutch. In the peace negotiations at Cologne in 1673 the Dutch protested that no treaty between England and any other power 'n'ait meslé la Mer Britannique avec celle du septentrion' (*Verbaal der Amb.* 1673/74). The English popular view of the question appears clearly in an anonymous pamphlet, *The Dutch Drawn to the Life*, published in 1664, just before the outbreak of the Second Dutch War. The writer speaks of 'the command of the Narrow Sea, the Dutch coast and ours' (p. 53); and again, referring to the action taken by King Charles I in 1640 (p. 148), 'When our neighbours the Dutchmen minded their interest and were almost Masters at Sea in the Northern Fishing... upon our Fishmongers' complaint the King encouraged several overtures and projects concerning Busses for our own Coasts service, the prevention of strangers, and the improvement of the Narrow Seas, &c.'

C. THE JÜLICH-CLEVES SUCCESSION QUESTION.

The death of John William (March 9, 1609), the mad Duke of Jülich-Cleves, without issue, raised the important question of the succession to his territory, which lay astride the Rhine on the eastern frontier of the United Provinces. It was felt to be essential for the protection of Protestant interests in Germany and the Netherlands that the Duchies should not fall into the hands of a partisan of the house of Habsburg. Duke John William had four sisters, but only the claims of the descendants of the two eldest really counted. Maria Eleanora had married Duke Albert Frederick of Prussia. All her sons, however, had died young, but it was held that her claims had passed to the son of her daughter Anna, who had married John Sigismund, Elector of Brandenburg. This was disputed by the Count Palatine, Philip Lewis of Neuburg, who had married the second sister of the deceased duke, also named Anna. Eventually the Elector and the Count Palatine agreed to occupy the disputed territory jointly, and were known as 'the Possessors'. The Dutch recognized the title of 'the Possessors', but the Emperor Rudolph refused to do so, and with his sanction the Archduke Leopold, Bishop of Passau, at the head of an armed force, made his way into the Duchies and seized the fortress of Jülich. Henry IV of France, who had been meditating an expedition for the overthrow of the Habsburg power, seized the opportunity for planning a great alliance with the Dutch, James I of England, and the Protestant princes of Germany for the expulsion of the Archduke and the recovering of Jülich. His assassination, May 14, 1610, put an end to his ambitious schemes, but though deprived of the help of a great French army, Maurice of Nassau, at the head of a considerable force of Dutch and English troops, entered the Duchies and was joined by the troops of the 'Possessing' princes. On September 1, Jülich surrendered, and Archduke Leopold left the territory. The troubles were not, however, yet over. The 'Possessors', as perhaps might have been expected, quarrelled. John Sigismund of Brandenburg became a Calvinist, Wolfgang William of Neuburg married the sister of the Duke of Bavaria, and announced his conversion to Catholicism. In September, 1614, Maurice of Nassau, with Dutch troops, and Spinola at the head of a Spanish force, both entered the Duchies, and a hostile encounter seemed inevitable. Hostilities were, however, avoided, and by the treaty of Xanten (November 12) the two rivals agreed to a partition of the territory.

D. THE ORIGIN AND EARLY HISTORY OF THE FELLOWSHIP OF THE MERCHANT ADVENTURERS.

The Fellowship of Merchant Adventurers has the distinction of holding the first place, not only in England, but in Western and Central Europe, as the pioneer of great trading corporations. The Gilds of the Middle Ages were municipal and local institutions. The Hansa League in Germany was a bond, not between merchants dealing in particular wares, but between a group of towns.

England in the fourteenth century had no manufactures. Her only industries were cattle-breeding and agriculture; her exports were raw materials, chiefly wool. English wool was famed for its quality, and was much sought after by the cloth weavers of the Netherlands, Germany, and Italy. The trade was almost entirely in the hands of the Hansa and of Italians, who sent over agents to England to buy up the wool and export it to the Continent. In England itself, before a.d. 1300, the sale of the best wool, that of the royal flocks and of the great landowners, was conducted under the royal licence by an official body or group of merchants, known as 'Merchants of the Staple'. A Staple (*stabile emporium*) was a place set apart for the export and import of certain articles; and there were ten or a dozen English towns, known as Staple Towns— among them Newcastle, York, Norwich, Westminster, and Bristol—where alone the wool traffic could be carried on. Also on the Continent there was a Staple Town, which was the recognized centre of the foreign trade, having exclusive rights. No wool could legally be shipped from England to any other port. During almost the whole of the fourteenth century the Staple was at Bruges. The institution by Philip the Good, Duke of Burgundy, of the famous Order of the Golden Fleece, at Bruges in 1430, had a direct reference to the English wool, which had so much contributed to the town's prosperity. By that date, however, a change had already taken place in England. Flemish refugees had, during the troubled times of the Arteveldes, fled across the Channel, taking with them their skill in the textile industries. Many of them settled at Norwich, then one of the Staple towns, and introduced the art of cloth-weaving. Only the coarser fabrics, rough white cloths, baize, and kersey, were produced, and these were sent over to Ghent, Bruges, Ypres, and other places, to be finished and dyed. To a monopoly of this trade the Staple Company, which had in 1359 removed from Bruges to Calais, had no claim, and the exporting of cloth fell into other hands. Enterprising English traders, under the name of Merchant Adventurers, had already begun to visit foreign countries with their wares, the pioneers of a commerce which was one day to encircle the world. Their first official recognition came from the Kings of the house of Lancaster. By a letter patent of Henry IV, 1407, they were granted the privilege of appointing a governor or consul to represent them in certain towns, where they traded. Their consolidation into an organized society appears to have been a gradual process, and little is known of the actual steps by which the court or central governing body of the Merchant Adventurers came into being, but in the middle of the fifteenth century it was in existence, and at the same time Antwerp became the port to which exclusively their goods were sent and from which they were distributed to other parts of the continent—in other words, their Staple. At Antwerp a wharf, warehouse, and dwellings were erected for their use, and extensive privileges granted to them, including a certain autonomous jurisdiction.

The Charter which constituted them into an organized corporation was granted by Henry VI in 1462. By this Charter the Fellowship obtained the monopoly of the trade in woollen goods, at least all traders who were not members of the Fellowship had to pay a tax for their privilege, low at first, but which at the end of the century had risen so high as to be practically prohibitive. By this Charter the right of jurisdiction at Antwerp was confirmed and placed in the hands of a court consisting of a governor and twelve assistants, the governor being appointed by the King, the assistants elected by the members. Shortly after the granting of this Charter the activity of the Adventurers at Antwerp aroused the hostility of the Flemish weavers, and Duke Philip the Good was induced by their complaints to forbid in 1464 the importation of English woollen goods into his dominion. They had therefore for awhile to withdraw to Utrecht. On Philip's death in 1467 the interdict was removed, and Antwerp again became the Staple of the Adventurers, and was to be their home for wellnigh two centuries.

The period of the greatest prosperity of the Fellowship was the sixteenth century, the period of the Tudors. This prosperity was built up on the privileges and monopoly granted to them by the Charter of Henry VII in 1501, which was extended in 1505 and remained in force until the reign of James I. The governing body consisted of a governor and twenty-four assistants, elected by the 'General Court', as the whole assembly of members was styled. This governing body had extensive powers, legislative, executive, and judicial. Their jurisdiction over the members was not confined to civil actions, but they had the power of inflicting heavy fines and even imprisonment for criminal offences. To become a member—'a free and sworn brother'—of the Fellowship an apprenticeship of not less than eight years had to be served, except in the case of sons of members; and proof had to be given of English birth and parentage. A 'brother' who married a foreigner or acquired foreign property was disqualified.

Four times a year the ships of the Fellowship gathered at London and sailed to Antwerp, carrying a cargo of half-finished white cloths, kerseys, and baize. The merchants themselves had to accompany their goods, for it was prescribed 'that every one must sell his own wares'. These sales could only take place in the Court-house, and only three times a week, on Mondays, Wednesdays, and Fridays. The carrying out of these regulations and jurisdiction within the Staple was entrusted to a secondary governing body or court consisting, like the head body in London, of an elected governor and assistants. The great rival of the Adventurers had been the Staple Company and the Hansa League, but both these bodies became in the sixteenth century decadent, and with the capture of Calais in 1558 the Staple Company ceased to exist. But though the loss of Calais made Antwerp more than ever the centre of the English continental trade, troubles were in store for the Merchant Adventurers.

With the accession of Elizabeth disputes arose between the English and Spanish Governments about the interpretation of the treaty of commerce, known as the *Magnus Intercursus*, concluded in 1496 between Henry VII and Philip the Fair. Margaret of Parma, the Governor of the Netherlands, took in 1563 the strong step of forbidding the entrance of English goods into the Netherlands. Elizabeth replied by closing the English harbours to ships from the Netherlands. For about a year this state of things spelt ruin to the Adventurers, but no less so to Antwerp. In 1564, accordingly, an understanding was reached, and the Court once more returned to its old quarters on the Scheldt. But for a brief space only. The outbreak of the Revolt led to the banishment of the Adventurers from the Netherlands, and at the end of 1564 they left Antwerp finally.

Shut out from the Netherlands, the Fellowship now tried to set up their Staple further north in the region dominated by their chief rivals the Hansa League. At first they found a resting-place at Emden, but in 1567 they were tempted by an invitation from Hamburg to set up their Court in that great seaport, from whence by the Elbe they had access to the German market. Hamburg thus played for its own profit the part of traitor to the League, of which it was one of the foremost members. The residence at Hamburg lasted ten years, but the bitter opposition of the Hansa to their presence proved too strong, and by an Imperial decree of Rudolph II they were in 1577 banished from German soil. The energies of the Adventurers were now diverted into different channels, small factories being placed at Stade, Emden, and even at Elbing near Dantzic. A more important move was the attempt to re-enter the Netherlands by the erection of a subsidiary court at Middelburg in 1582. Holland and Zeeland had now practically freed themselves from Spanish rule, and Middelburg, on the island of Walcheren, was the capital of Zeeland, and at that time a flourishing port. With the growth of the United Provinces in power and wealth, it was clearly the best policy of the Fellowship to establish its chief Staple and Court within the boundaries of the Republic. There were many claimants, among them Groningen, Delft, and Rotterdam. But after many negotiations, an influential deputation sent by Middelburg in January, 1598, to London, decided the choice of the English Government and of the General Court of the Adventurers in favour of making this town their sole Staple upon the Continent, and the seat of their Great Court. Many points concerning the rights and privileges to be enjoyed, together with the restrictions imposed, were the subject of much discussion before the terms of the agreement was finally settled between the town of Middelburg, the States of Zeeland, and the States-General on the one hand, and the English Privy Council and the governing body of the Fellowship on the other. The principal conditions were that the Adventurers should carry on their entire business within the Republic at the one Staple-town, and all English subjects were forbidden to bring woollen goods to any other port of the United Provinces. Their later history is told in the lectures that precede. The Staple and Court remained at Middelburg from 1598 to 1621; at Delft from 1621 to 1634; at Rotterdam from 1634 to 1656; at Dordrecht from 1656 to 1665. After the close of the Second English War the States-General in 1668 refused to grant the Adventurers their old privileges, and the long connexion with the Netherlands ceased.

E. THE INTERLOPERS.

This name for the smugglers who, despite the exclusive rights of the Merchant Adventurers, carried English woollen goods to other Dutch ports than the privileged Staple, was derived from the Dutch term *inter*-or *entre-loopers*, i. e. 'runners-in'. During the whole time that the Court and Staple were at Middelburg, the port of Flushing, only a few miles distant on the same island of Walcheren, was in English hands, being one of the so-called 'cautionary' towns, which were a pledge to Queen Elizabeth for the repayment of her loans, and were garrisoned by English troops. Flushing was during this period a centre of smuggling, and the Flushing 'interlopers' a great annoyance to the Adventurers. The smuggling went on, however, with activity after the retrocession of Flushing in 1616, especially to the port of Amsterdam. The powerful Amsterdam merchants, who profited by the illicit trade, did their utmost to encourage the 'interlopers', and to protect them in spite of the angry protests of the Adventurers, and of the corporations of the interested Staple-towns.

The word 'interlopers' was soon universally applied to all private traders who trespassed against the privileges of a Chartered Company, more especially in the East

Indies.

Bodies of English volunteers were to be found fighting under the Prince of Orange against the Spaniards from the very beginning of the Dutch War of Independence. In 1572 a force of 1,500 men under Sir Humphrey Gilbert landed at Flushing, with the connivance of Queen Elizabeth, and from this time forward English troops took part in all the fiercest fighting. In 1571 there were four English regiments in the field, commanded by Colonels Norris, Cavendish, Cotton, and Morgan. During the time of Leicester's Governor-Generalship, 1585-7, the number of the English army in the Netherlands amounted to 8,000 men, horse and foot. After his departure, a considerable though reduced force was left under the command of Lord Willoughby. In 1589 he was succeeded in this post by the famous Sir Francis Vere, the hero of the battle of Nieuport, 1600, and of the siege of Ostend, 1601-4, and many another desperate struggle. It was during the time of his command that in 1595 an arrangement was made between the States-General and Queen Elizabeth, by the terms of which the English troops were henceforth to enter the service of the States and receive Dutch pay. The English Government allowed them to be recruited in England, and they were to wear distinctive English uniforms, carry English colours, and have their own national march and beat of the drum, but were to take during their service an oath of allegiance to the States-General from whom the officers received their commissions. The number was fixed at 4,000.

Sir Francis Vere was followed in the command by his younger brother Sir Horace Vere, afterwards Lord Vere of Tilbury, in 1608. During the twelve years' truce, 1609-21, the English regiments were retained in the service of the States, and in 1610 under Sir Edward Cecil, afterwards Lord Wimbledon, distinguished themselves at the siege of Jülich. From the outbreak of the war again in 1621 to the peace of Munster in 1648, the English regiments took part in all the campaigns of Maurice (died 1625) and of Frederick Henry, Prince of Orange. In 1622 the names of the four Colonels were Edward Vere, Edward Cecil, Charles Morgan, and Edward Harwood. On them and the Scottish Brigade always fell the brunt of the fighting. They particularly distinguished themselves in the defence of Bergen-op-zoom (1622), and in the capture of Hertogenbosch (1622), of Maestricht (1632), and of Breda (1637). In 1626, the army of Frederick Henry included 14,500 English troops and 5,000 Scottish. At Hertogenbosch, Colonel Sir Edward Vere was killed; at Maestricht, Colonel Sir Edward Harwood and the Earl of Oxford; at Breda, Colonels Sir Charles Morgan and Goring were wounded. In 1644, the names of the four Colonels were Craven, Cromwell, Herbert, and Goring.

After the peace of Munster (1648), followed in 1650 by the death of the Stadholder William II, the republican party in the States, now predominant, resolved to reduce the number of their standing army, but the English regiments were retained until the outbreak of the war with the Commonwealth, when they were all disbanded. In 1656, however, when peace had been restored, a single regiment was recruited from the veterans, who had remained in Holland, chiefly royalist refugees, and it was henceforth known as the Holland regiment. The command was conferred on Colonel John Cromwell, a cousin of the Protector, but a stanch loyalist.

On the declaration of war between England and the United Provinces in 1665, the Holland regiment was summoned home. It became the 4th Regiment of Foot, but still retained its old name, the Holland Regiment, until 1689. In that year William III changed its title to 'Prince George of Denmark's Regiment', and it became the 3rd Foot. On the death of Prince George in 1708, their style was once more altered, and this time, from the colour of their waistcoats, breeches, and stockings, they were styled 'the Buffs,' a name they were to retain until our own day. They are now the East Kent Regiment.

Not less interesting, and even more prolonged, is the story of the Scottish regiments in the Netherlands. The first record of Scottish volunteers is in 1573. From 1603 to 1628 there were two regiments. After 1628 there were three, except during the reign of William III, when their number was increased. The group of regiments was always known as the Scots Brigade, and it was continuously in the Dutch service receiving Dutch pay for more than two centuries, except the decade 1688-98, when, under the Dutch King of Great Britain, they received British pay. Even during the Anglo-Dutch wars of 1653, 1665, and 1672 they were not disbanded, but were converted for the time into Dutch regiments, and in consequence of this their composition during this period became considerably leavened with an admixture of foreigners. Of the Scots who remained, it must always be remembered that a number of them had been settled in the Netherlands for two or three generations. After 1674 their thoroughly Scottish character was restored. From that date until 1781 the Scots Brigade remained in Holland. But when Great Britain declared war against the United Provinces in that year, the question of the position of the Scottish regiments was raised, and the States-General resolved that they should be completely denationalized and the officers be required to take an oath abjuring allegiance to their own country. The large majority at once threw up their commissions, and the Scots Brigade in the Dutch service ceased to exist. The subsequent history is curious. In 1794 the Scots Brigade was by order of the British Government reformed. In 1803 its strength was reduced, and the 'Brigade' became the 94th Regiment. Until 1809 the 94th wore Highland dress, but this was then discontinued. The regiment, however, retained the green facings which they had inherited from one of the Dutch regiments. Disbanded in 1818, but reconstituted in 1878, the facings remained green, and a diced band round the shako still proclaimed the Scottish connexion. Its last service as the 94th was in the Boer War of 1880, when a part of the regiment when on march in time of peace was suddenly attacked at

Bronker's Spruit, and had heavy losses. The army reorganization of 1881 led to the 94th becoming the battalion linked to the 88th, an Irish regiment, probably for no other reason than the green facing. The glorious Scottish tradition therefore of three centuries was henceforth lost, and the regiment which represented the Scots Brigade became the 2nd battalion of the Connaught Rangers, with its head-quarters at Galway.

G. KING CHARLES'S PROCLAMATION FOR THE RESTRAINT OF FISHING UPON HIS MAIESTIES SEAS AND COASTS WITHOUT LICENCE (1636).

Whereas our Father of blessed memory King James did in the seuenth yeere of His reigne of Great Brittaine, set forth a Proclamation touching Fishing; whereby for the many important reasons therein expressed, all persons of what Nation or quality soeuer (being not His naturall borne Subjects) were restrained from Fishing vpon any the Coasts and Seas of Great Brittaine, Ireland and the rest of the Isles adjacent, where most vsually heretofore Fishing had been, vntill they had orderly demanded, and obtained Licences from Our said Father or His Commissioners in that behalfe, vpon paine of such chastisement as should be fit to be inflicted vpon such wilfull Offenders: Since which time, albeit neither Our said Father, nor Our Selfe haue made any considerable execution of the said Proclamation, but haue with much patience expected a voluntary conformity of Our Neighbours and Allies to so iust and reasonable Prohibitions and Directions as are contained in the same.

And now finding by experience, that all the inconueniences which occasioned that Proclamation, are rather increased than abated: We being very sensible of the premisses, and well knowing how farre we are obliged in Honour to maintaine the rights of our Crowne, especially of so great consequence, haue thought it necessary, by the aduice of Our priuie Councell, to renew the aforesaid restraint of Fishing vpon Our aforesaid Coasts and Seas, without Licence first obtained from Us, and by these presents to make publique Declaration, that Our resolution is (at times conuenient) to keepe such a competent strength of Shipping vpon Our Seas, as may (by God's blessing) be sufficient, both to hinder such further encroachments vpon Our Regalities, and assist and protect those Our good Friends and Allies, who shall henceforth, by vertue of Our Licences (to be first obtained) endeauour to take the benefit of Fishing vpon Our Coasts and Seas, in the places accustomed.

Giuen at Our Palace of Westminster the tenth day of May, in the twelfth yeere of Our Reigne of England, Scotland, France, and Ireland.

God saue the King.

BIBLIOGRAPHY

PRINTED BOOKS AND PAMPHLETS

AITZEMA, L. Saken van Staet en Oorlogh in en omtrent de Vereenigte Nederlanden, 1621-68. 6 vols. fol., The Hague, 1669-71.

ALBÈRI, E. Relazioni degli ambasciatori veneti. Ser. iv, Inghilterra. Florence, 1846-62.

BEAUJON, A. Overzicht der Geschiedenis van de Nederlandsche Zeevisscherijen. Leiden, 1885.

BIRDWOOD, SIR G., and FOSTER, W. The first letter-book of the East India Company, 1600-19. London, 1893.

BLOK, P. J. Geschiedenis der Nederlandsche Volk. Vol. iv, Groningen, 1899.

BOROUGH, SIR JOHN. The Soveraignty of the British seas (written 1633). London, 1651.

BRUGMANS, H. Engeland en de Nederlanden in de eerste Jaren van Elizabeth's regeering, 1558-67. Groningen, 1892.

CARLETON, SIR DUDLEY. Letters from and to during his embassy in Holland, 1616-21, and State letters during his embassy, 1627. London, 1841.

—— Lettres, Mémoires et négotiations dans le temps de son ambassade en Hollande, 1616-20. 3 vols., The Hague, 1758.

CLARENDON, EDWARD, EARL OF. State papers collected by. 3 vols., Oxford, 1767-86.

—— History of the Rebellion. 6 vols., Oxford, 1888.

COMMELIN, IZ. Begin en Voortgangh van de Vereen-Geoct: Oost-Indische Compagnie. 2 vols., Amsterdam, 1646.

DIGGES, SIR D. Defence of Trade. London, 1615.

Dutch, The. Drawn to the life. London, 1664.

FERGUSON, JAMES. Scots Brigade in Holland. 3 vols., Edinburgh, 1899.

FORTESCUE, J. W. History of the British Army. Vol. i, London, 1899.

FRUIN, R. Verspreide Geschriften. 10 vols., The Hague, 1905.

—— Tien Jaren uit den Tachtigjarigen Oorlog. The Hague, 1899.

GARDINER, S. R. History of England from the accession of James I to the outbreak of the Civil War, 1603-42. 10 vols., London, 1883-4.

—— Letters and Papers relating to the first Dutch War. Published for the Navy Records Society, 1898.

GEDDES, J. The Administration of John De Witt, 1625-54. London, 1879.

GENTLEMAN, TOBIAS. England's Way to Win Wealth, pp. 378-91, vol. iii, Harleian Misc. (see below).

GRAVIÈRE, J. DE LA. Les Anglais et les Hollandais dans les mers polaires et dans la mer des Indes. Paris, 1890.

GROEN V. PRINSTERER, G. Archives ou Correspondance de la Maison d'Orange-Nassau, 2nd series. 5 vols., Utrecht, 1841-61.

GROTIUS, HUGO. Mare Liberum. Leiden, 1633.

Harleian Miscellany. 10 vols., London, 1808.

JONGE, J. C. DE. Geschiedenis van het Nederlandsche Zeewesen. 6 vols., The Hague, 1833-48.

JONGE, J. K. J. DE. De Opkomst van het Nederl. Gezag in Oost-Indie. 13 vols., The Hague, 1862-89.

J. R. The Trades Increase. pp. 202-20, vol. iv, Harleian Misc. (see above).

KNIGHT, H. R. Historical records of the Buffs, 3rd. Foot, formerly designated The Holland Regiment. London, 1905.

KRONICK van het historisch Genootschap te Utrecht, 1869. Brieven van de Gezanten in Engeland Joachimi, Boreel en J. V. Rheede, 1642-50.

LINGELBACK, W. E. The Merchant Adventurers of England, their Laws and Ordinances. Philadelphia, 1903.

LINTUM, C. E. De Merchant Adventurers in de Nederlanden. The Hague, 1905.

LUZAC, E. Hollands Rijkdom, behoudende den oorsprong van den Koophandel en de Magt van dezen Staat. 4 vols., Leiden, 1781.

MACPHERSON, D. Annals of Commerce. 4 vols., London, 1805.

—— History of the European Commerce with India. London, 1812.

MITZUKURI, G. Englisch-Niederländische Unionsbestrebungen im Zeitalter Cromwells. Tübingen, 1891.

MULLER FZ, S. Geschiedenis der Noordsche Compagnie. Utrecht, 1874.

—— Mare Clausum, Bijdrage tot de Geschiedenis der Rivaliteit van Engeland en Nederland in de 17e eeuw. Amsterdam, 1872.

OPPENHEIM, M. History of the administration of the Royal Navy and of Merchant Shipping in relation to the Navy, 1509-1660. London, 1893.

OVERBURY, SIR T. Observations in his travels. Vol. viii, Harleian Misc.

RALEIGH, SIR W. Works. 8 vols., Oxford, 1829.

—— Observations touching trade and commerce with the Hollanders. pp. 351-76. Vol. viii.

—— A discourse of the invention of ships, &c., pp. 317-34. Vol. viii.

RANKE, L. VON. A history of England, principally in the 17th century (Eng. tr.). 6 vols., Oxford, 1875.

REES, O. VAN. Geschied. der Stadhuiskunde in Nederland tot het einde der 18e eeuw. 2 vols., Utrecht, 1868.

SELDEN, JOHN. Mare Clausum seu de Dominio Maris. Libri duo, London, 1635.

TIDEMAN, M. C. De Zee Betwist. Geschiedenis der onderhandelingen over der Zeeheerschappij tusschen de Engelsche Republiek en de Vereenigte Provincien voor den eersten Zee-Oorlog. Dordrecht, 1876.

THURLOE, JOHN. A collection of the State Papers of. 7 vols., London, 1742.

VREEDE, G. W. Inleiding tot eene Geschiedenis der Nederlandsche Diplomatie. 6 vols., Utrecht, 1856-65.

—— Nederland en Cromwell. Utrecht, 1853.

WAGENAAR, J. Vaderlandsche historie. 21 vols., Amsterdam, 1754.

WELWOD, D. Abridgement of all Sea-Lawes. London, 1613.

WELWOOD, J. Memoirs of the most material transactions of England for the 100 years preceding the Revolution of 1688. London, 1820.

WHITELOCKE, B. Memorials. 4 vols., Oxford, 1853.

WINWOOD, SIR R. Memorials of affairs of State in the Reigns of Queen Elizabeth and King James I. 3 vols., London, 1725.

ZORGDRAGER, D. Bloeijende Opkomst der Aloude en Hedendaagsche Groenlandsche Visscherij. The Hague, 1727.

FOOTNOTES

[1]See the admirable monograph on the subject by the late Professor Robert Fruin, *Tien Jaren uit de Tachtigjarigen Oorlog, 1588-98.*

[2]The towns of Flushing and Brill and the fort of Rammekens were delivered into the hands of Elizabeth, as security for repayment.

[3]Res. Holl. June 12, 1609.

[4]Res. St.-Gen. June 12, 1609.

[5]Art. 6 of the Treaty between James and the States, July 6 (June 25, 1609, o.s.).

[6]Winwood, *Memorials*, vol. iii.

[7]The Zeelanders in the seventeenth century, though they sent out many fishermen to the Dogger Bank, to Greenland and Spitzbergen, did not take much part in the herring fishery. See note.

[8]Groot Placaet-Boek (July 19, 1606).

[9] *A Pollitique Platt*, by Robert Hitchcock, 1580.

Observations made upon the Dutch fishery about the year 1601, by John Keymer. Ralegh, *Works*, i. 144.

Sir Thomas Overbury's observations in his travels in 1609: *Harleian Misc.* viii. 349.

Discourse addressed to the King by Sir Nicholas Hales, on the benefit derived by the Dutch from English fisheries. Terms suggested for granting them a licence to fish for twenty-one years. *Calendar of State Papers, Dom. Ser., 1603-10*, p. 509.

[10] *Cal. State Papers, Dom. Ser., 1603-10*, p. 509.

[11] *Statutes of the Realm*, iv. 2, p. 1058.

[12]Letter of Salisbury to Cornwallis, June 8, 1609. Winwood's *State Papers*, iii. 44-50.

[13]Fruin's *Verspreide Geschriften*, vol. iii, pp. 408-45.

[14]Winwood's *Memorials*, March 16, (o.s.), 1610. See also letter of April 6 (o.s.).

[15]See Note C.

[16] *Relazioni venete, Inghilterra*, serie iv, p. 128.

[17]See Note A.

[18]Ralegh's *Works*, viii. 351-76.

[19]See Note B.

[20]See Note.

[21] *Harleian Misc.* iii, pp. 397-8.

[22] *Ibid.* iv, pp. 212-31.

[23] *Relazioni Venete, Inghilterra*, iv. 206.

[24]Ranke, *Hist. of England* (Oxf. trans.), i. 473.

[25]Dated Jan. 6/16. Letters to and from Sir Dudley Carleton during his embassy in Holland from January 1615/16, to December 1620. London, 1757.

[26]Greenland here stands for Spitzbergen. All through these disputes, owing to geographical ignorance, the two terms are used almost interchangeably.

[27]Aitzema *Saken van Staet en Oorlog*, ii. 356.

[28]See Note D.

[29]See Note E.

[30]Carleton's letters during his embassy in Holland, January 1615/16, to December 1620, p. 111.

[31]Carleton's *Letters*, pp. 156-7. Report of the Lords of the Council with the King in Scotland, to the Lords of the Council in England, Aug. 4/14, 1617.

[32]Carleton's *Letters*, October 11.

[33]The Governor-General, Jan Pietersz Coen.

[34]See special note F.

[35] *Cambridge Modern History*, iv. 758.

[36]The orthography of the original.

[37]Sir Dudley Carleton's *State Letters*, 1627, pp. 5-15.

[38]See note G.

[39] *Rikskansleren Axel Oxenstierna's Skrifter och Brefvexling, Hugo Grotii bref*, ii. 1633-9, pp. 335-58.

[40] *Grotii bref*, April 9, 1639, p. 595, 'video cum dolore inter Anglos et Gallos veteres recrudescere inimicitias.'

[41] *Grotii bref*, April 23, 1639, p. 602, 'Haud equidem affirmaverim, quod suspicantur Angli, Gallicis pecuniis sustentari Scoticam factionem pauperiorem ceteroqui quam ut bello diu sufficiat. Creduntur autem id facere Galli, non tantum ex aemulatu vetere, verum etiam quod cum Batavi nunc consilia socient ad capienda Flandriae oppida maritima, quod cum solus prohibere possit Anglus, domestico ob id negotio distinendus sit.'

[42] *Archives de la Maison d'Orange-Nassau*, 2nd ser., iii. 171, 'dès aussitôt que j'auray endormi le faict des Duyns, qui est le seul object de ma commission.'

[43] *Archives de la Maison d'Orange-Nassau*, 2nd ser., iii. 200, 201.

[44] *Clarendon State Papers*, ii. 71.

[45]Ranke, *Englische Geschichte*, ii. 362.

[46] *Archives*, 2nd series, iii. 381.

[47] *History of the Rebellion*, v. 418.

[48]Among them Prince Edward, son of the Queen of Bohemia.

[49]'Placaet ende Ordonnantie op 't stuk van den Haring-Vaert, 't branden van de tonnen en 't soorten van den Haringh.' *Derde Memoriael boek 's Hof v. Holland.*

CPSIA information can be obtained at www.ICGtesting.com
Printed in the USA
LVOW04s0340120815

449704LV00030B/1408/P